ELEPHANT ADVENTURE

A KID'S GUIDE TO THE WORLD'S GENTLE GIANTS

BRIAN THOMAS

Copyright © 2024 by Brian Thomas

All rights reserved.

No part of this book may be reproduced in any form or by any electronic or mechanical means, including information storage and retrieval systems, without written permission from the author, except for the use of brief quotations in a book review.

INTRODUCTION: WHY ELEPHANTS ARE AMAZING

Elephants are incredible creatures. Imagine standing next to an animal so big that its shoulder reaches higher than the tallest basketball player's head. Now picture that this giant isn't just powerful but also gentle, wise, and playful. That's an elephant. They're not only the largest land animals on Earth, but they're also some of the most fascinating.

One thing that makes elephants so special is how they seem to understand the world around them. People often say elephants never forget, and there's truth to that. In fact, elephants have memories that help them remember places, other elephants, and even humans they've met before. Scientists have studied elephants for years and discovered that their brains are highly developed, especially in areas connected to emotions, learning, and problem-solving. Imagine being able to solve puzzles or remember exactly where to find water, even if you haven't been to that place in years. That's just an ordinary day for an elephant.

Elephants also have families that are just as interesting as their brains. They live in groups called herds, led by the oldest female, known as the matriarch. She's like the wise grandmother who knows everything about the land, where to find food, and how to keep everyone safe. The rest of the herd is usually made up of her daughters, sisters, and their calves. Together, they form a tight-knit team, looking out for each other and protecting the little ones. It's not just survival; it's love and teamwork.

What's truly amazing is how elephants communicate with each other. You've probably heard their trumpeting calls in movies or on TV, but that's only part of the story. Elephants use low rumbling sounds that humans can barely hear. These rumbles travel through the ground and can be picked up by other elephants' feet miles away! It's like having a secret long-distance phone call. They use these sounds to warn each other of danger, find lost herd members, or even greet friends they haven't seen in years.

But communication isn't just about sounds. Elephants are also experts at reading body language. They flap their ears, use their trunks, or lean against each other to show how they're feeling. Sometimes, elephants even cry. That's right—elephants shed tears when they're upset, and they comfort each other in times of sadness. It's one of the many ways they show their emotional depth. They've been known to mourn their dead, returning to the same spot year after year to touch the bones of a lost friend or family member. Doesn't that make them seem almost human in a way?

Their trunks are another feature that makes elephants stand out. An elephant's trunk isn't just a nose; it's also a hand, a tool, and even a snorkel. With more than 40,000 muscles, an elephant's trunk is incredibly strong and flexible. It can pick up something as heavy as a tree branch or as delicate as a single blade of grass. Elephants use their trunks to eat, drink, smell, and even play. Baby elephants, just like human toddlers, have to learn how to use their trunks properly. Sometimes, they swing them around or even trip over them. It's both adorable and a reminder that even the biggest animals start small.

When it comes to eating, elephants are champions. They need a lot of food to keep their huge bodies going —hundreds of pounds every day! From grass to fruits, bark, and leaves, an elephant's diet is as diverse as the landscapes they roam. But elephants don't just eat for themselves. In the wild, they play a vital role in shaping their environment. As they travel, they knock down trees, dig for water, and spread seeds through their dung. Yes, even elephant poop is important—it helps grow new plants and trees, keeping the ecosystem healthy.

Elephants are also remarkable swimmers. You might not expect an animal of their size to love the water, but they do. In fact, elephants are excellent swimmers and can use their trunks like snorkels to breathe while crossing rivers. Watching an elephant splash around is like seeing pure joy in action. They'll spray water with their trunks, roll in the mud, and even slide down riverbanks. It's fun for them and helpful, too—mud baths keep their skin healthy and protect them from sunburn and insect bites.

Perhaps one of the most amazing things about elephants is their connection to people. In many cultures, elephants are symbols of strength, wisdom, and luck. For centuries, humans and elephants have worked together. In places like India and Thailand, elephants have helped carry heavy loads, build roads, and even participate in religious ceremonies. Unfortunately, this relationship hasn't always been fair to the elephants. Some have been mistreated or forced to live in poor conditions. Thankfully, more people are working today to protect them and ensure they are treated with respect.

In the wild, elephants face challenges, too. Their habitats are shrinking as humans build cities, farms, and roads where elephants once roamed freely. Poachers hunt elephants for their tusks, which are made of ivory. This has caused elephant populations to drop in some areas. Despite these challenges, elephants are survivors. With the help of conservationists and animal lovers, there's hope that these gentle giants will continue to thrive.

Elephants are more than just animals; they're a reminder of how incredible nature can be. They teach us about kindness, intelligence, and the importance of sticking together. Whether they're sharing a special moment with their herd, finding water in the middle of a drought, or simply enjoying a swim, elephants show us what it means to live fully and care deeply.

The importance of elephants

In the wild, elephants act like gardeners for their habitats. They shape their environment in ways that help countless other species survive. Picture a forest. Without elephants, it would look very different. When elephants eat fruit and other plants, they scatter seeds far and wide through their dung. These seeds grow into new plants and trees, creating food and shelter for birds, insects, and other animals. This is why elephants are sometimes called "ecosystem engineers." It's a big name, but it fits them perfectly because they literally build and maintain their environments.

Their role doesn't stop with planting trees. Elephants also create pathways through thick forests and tall grasses. As they walk, they knock down bushes and trample grass, which opens up trails that smaller animals, like antelopes and even humans, use to move around. These paths can also lead to hidden waterholes that other animals might not find on their own. Elephants share their discoveries without even realizing it, helping everyone from lions to tiny frogs survive in tough conditions.

Water is another area where elephants shine. In dry seasons, elephants often dig into riverbeds with their trunks to find water underground. These wells don't just help the elephants; they provide drinking water for all kinds of animals. Imagine being a thirsty zebra or a warthog on a hot day and suddenly finding a pool of fresh water, thanks to an elephant's hard work. It's like nature's version of teamwork, where the elephant leads the way.

This connection between elephants and their environment is something scientists are still trying to fully understand. What's clear is that elephants keep the balance in their habitats. Without them, entire ecosystems could collapse. For example, in parts of Africa where elephant populations have decreased, forests have started to shrink because fewer seeds are being spread. This affects not just plants but also animals that depend on those plants for food and shelter. When elephants thrive, the whole ecosystem benefits.

Beyond their physical impact on nature, elephants are deeply important to many human cultures. Across Africa and Asia, elephants are symbols of strength, wisdom, and even good luck. In some countries, elephants are seen as sacred animals. In India, for instance, there's a famous god named Ganesha who has the head of an elephant. People pray to Ganesha for help with new beginnings, success, and removing obstacles. Can you imagine having an elephant-headed god as a symbol of hope and wisdom? It shows just how much elephants mean to people.

In Thailand, elephants have been called the "national animal" because they've been part of the country's history and culture for centuries. They appear in old stories, on coins, and even on flags. Long ago, Thai kings used elephants in battles because of their incredible strength and intelligence. Today, people in Thailand celebrate elephants with festivals, like National Elephant Day, to remind everyone how special these animals are.

But elephants aren't just important in faraway places. They've left their mark on cultures all around the world. In Africa, elephants appear in folktales passed down from generation to generation. These stories often teach lessons about bravery, kindness, and respect for nature. For example, one popular story tells of a wise elephant who saves smaller animals from a dangerous predator, showing that size and strength should be used to help others, not harm them.

Even in modern times, elephants inspire people. They appear in books, movies, and art, reminding us of their beauty and intelligence. You've probably heard of Dumbo, the flying elephant, or seen elephants at the zoo. These moments help us feel connected to elephants, even if we've never seen one in the wild. They make us think about how we can protect these incredible creatures for future generations.

But the relationship between elephants and humans hasn't always been positive. For hundreds of years, people have hunted elephants for their ivory tusks. This has caused terrible harm to elephant populations. When elephants are killed for their tusks, it's not just the elephants who suffer. The entire ecosystem feels the impact, as we've already seen. Thankfully, many people around the world are working to stop this. Conservation efforts and laws banning the ivory trade are helping protect elephants, but there's still a long way to go.

One of the most inspiring things about elephants is how they bring people together. Across the globe, people are raising awareness about the importance of elephants and why they need our help. From schoolchildren writing letters to politicians to scientists dedicating their lives to studying elephants, there's a shared understanding that these animals are worth saving. This kind of teamwork shows how much elephants matter—not just in the wild but also in our hearts and minds.

Fun facts

An adult African elephant can weigh as much as 14,000 pounds. That's the same as about two pickup trucks or more than 100 average-sized kids combined! They can stand up to 13 feet tall at the shoulder, which is taller than the rim of a basketball hoop. Even Asian elephants, which are slightly smaller than their African relatives, are still huge, reaching heights of around 10 feet and weighing up to 11,000 pounds. It's hard to imagine something so massive walking around with such grace.

Their size is not just impressive—it's also vital to how they survive in the wild. Being large means that they have fewer natural predators. Lions and hyenas might try to attack a baby elephant, but no animal dares mess with a fully grown adult. Their size alone is a powerful form of protection, a reminder to other creatures that messing with an elephant is not a good idea.

But being the biggest isn't always easy. Elephants need a lot of food and water to keep their huge bodies going. An adult elephant eats up to 300 pounds of food every single day. Imagine having to eat that much! It's like eating 600 burgers in one day—though elephants stick to grass, leaves, fruits, and bark. They also drink up to 50 gallons of water daily, which is about the size of a large bathtub. This constant need for food and water means elephants spend most of their day looking for it. Their size helps them reach high branches or push over trees to get to the tastiest leaves, but it also means they can't live just anywhere. They need large areas with plenty of resources to survive.

Even their bones are enormous. An elephant's skull alone can weigh more than a fully grown adult human. Their legs are thick and sturdy, built to carry all that weight. Unlike humans, elephants walk on their toes, with a soft, spongy pad under their feet that helps support them and keep them quiet as they move. You might think such a big animal would be loud and clumsy, but elephants are surprisingly gentle and quiet when they walk. This is especially important in the wild, where they need to avoid being noticed by predators or even humans.

Another amazing thing about their size is how it affects their behavior. You might think such a big animal would be slow and lazy, but elephants are full of energy and curiosity. They travel long distances every day, looking for food, water, and safe places to rest. Sometimes, they walk up to 30 miles in a single day! Their size gives them the strength and stamina to keep going even in tough conditions, like during a drought when food and water are hard to find.

Their trunks, as you already know, are incredible tools, but their size makes them even more effective. An elephant's trunk can lift up to 600 pounds—that's about the weight of a motorcycle! They use their trunks to carry heavy objects, break branches, or even play with one another. Despite their size and strength, elephants are also capable of delicate movements, like picking up a single flower or gently touching another elephant's face.

Their tusks are another part of their incredible size. Made of ivory, these long, curved teeth can grow up to 10 feet long and weigh more than 200 pounds each. Elephants use their tusks for all kinds of tasks, from digging for water to defending themselves from threats. Sadly, these tusks are also the reason elephants are hunted by poachers, which puts them in great danger. Their size and power should protect them, but human greed has made their lives more difficult.

Interestingly, being the largest land animal means

elephants also have one of the longest lifespans in the animal kingdom. In the wild, elephants can live up to 60 or 70 years. That's about the same as humans! Their size allows them to grow slowly and live long lives, which is important for raising their young. Baby elephants stay with their mothers for years, learning everything they need to survive, from finding food to understanding herd dynamics. In a way, their size and long life give them the time to learn, grow, and become the wise, majestic creatures they are.

Elephants also use their size to help others in their herd. A large elephant can push a stuck baby out of the mud or defend the group from predators. They can even use their size to help smaller animals, like digging waterholes that other creatures can drink from. Their strength isn't just about survival—it's about sharing and caring, which is one of the many reasons elephants are so extraordinary.

Their massive size has also inspired awe and respect in human cultures for centuries. Ancient armies used elephants in battles, not just for their strength but also for the fear they could strike into their enemies. Imagine seeing a wall of elephants charging toward you—it would be terrifying! Thankfully, most elephants today aren't involved in battles, but they are still symbols of power and wisdom in many cultures.

1

MEET THE ELEPHANTS

Elephants are often thought of as one group of animals, but did you know there are actually two main species of elephants? These are the African elephant and the Asian elephant, and while they share a lot in common, they are also very different in some pretty fascinating ways. From their size and ears to their tusks and where they live, each species is unique, adapted perfectly to its own environment.

Let's start with the African elephant, the bigger of the two. African elephants can weigh up to 14,000 pounds and stand about 10 to 13 feet tall at the shoulder. That's taller than most one-story houses! Their massive size makes them the largest land animal on Earth, and they look the part, with wide bodies and long legs built to carry all that weight. But it's not just their size that sets them apart. African elephants have enormous ears, shaped almost like the continent of Africa if you look closely. These large ears aren't just for hearing—they help keep the elephants cool in the hot African sun. By flapping their ears, they create a breeze, almost like having built-in fans.

Now, let's take a look at Asian elephants. They're smaller, but only by elephant standards! They still weigh up to 11,000 pounds and stand about 8 to 10 feet tall at the shoulder. Their ears are much smaller than those of African elephants, rounded and more rectangular in shape. This difference has to do with where they live. Asian elephants are found in forests and grasslands in countries like India, Thailand, and Sri Lanka. The smaller ears are better suited to cooler, shaded environments, where they don't need as much help staying cool.

Another major difference between the two species is their tusks. Both male and female African elephants can have tusks, which they use for digging, stripping bark off trees, and defending themselves. Tusks are essentially long, curved teeth made of ivory, and they grow throughout an elephant's life. In Asian elephants, however, only some males have tusks. Females and some males have small, stubby teeth called tushes instead of full tusks. This makes it easy to tell the two species apart if you see them side by side.

If you look closely, you'll also notice differences in their trunks. Both African and Asian elephants have trunks that are incredibly strong and flexible, but the ends are a little different. African elephants have two finger-like extensions at the tip of their trunk, while

Asian elephants have just one. This small difference allows African elephants to pick up objects with more precision, almost like having a thumb and finger, while Asian elephants tend to scoop things up.

Habitat is another way the two species differ. African elephants roam across a wide range of landscapes, from the grassy savannas of Kenya to the dense rainforests of the Congo. This ability to thrive in different environments is part of what makes African elephants so remarkable. They can adapt to scorching heat, heavy rains, or dry, arid conditions. Asian elephants, on the other hand, are more specialized. They stick to forests and grasslands, often in areas with plenty of water. This difference in habitat also affects their behavior. African elephants tend to travel in larger herds and cover more ground, while Asian elephants stay in smaller groups and move shorter distances.

The way they interact with their surroundings is also influenced by their size and environment. African elephants are often called "ecosystem engineers" because they shape their habitats in major ways. By knocking down trees and trampling plants, they create open spaces that allow other animals to thrive. Their wide-ranging movements help spread seeds and nutrients across vast areas. Asian elephants, living in denser forests, play a slightly different role. They are like gardeners, carefully pruning the plants and helping the forest grow in a healthy, balanced way.

Even their social behavior shows subtle differences.

Both species live in matriarchal groups, meaning the oldest female leads the herd. This matriarch is responsible for guiding the herd to food and water and teaching younger elephants how to survive. In African elephants, the herds are usually larger and more tightly knit, with multiple generations of females and their calves staying together. Asian elephant herds are smaller and sometimes less connected, though they still have strong bonds within their group.

One thing both species share is their intelligence. Whether you're looking at an African elephant in the savanna or an Asian elephant in a forest, you'll notice they are incredibly curious and thoughtful. They use tools, solve problems, and show a wide range of emotions, from joy to sadness. Scientists have observed both species comforting each other during difficult times, mourning their dead, and even showing playful behavior, like sliding down hills or splashing in water.

Another shared challenge is the threat they face from humans. Both African and Asian elephants are endangered, though for slightly different reasons. African elephants are heavily affected by poaching, as their large tusks are targeted by ivory hunters. Asian elephants, with their smaller tusks, face different dangers, like habitat loss due to farming and deforestation. Learning about these differences helps us understand why both species need protection and how people around the world are working to help them.

Where elephants live

Elephants are found in some of the most fascinating places on Earth. These gentle giants roam across deserts, savannahs, forests, and even swamps, adapting to their surroundings in ways that make them true survivors. Imagine walking through these different landscapes and seeing how elephants thrive in each one. It's almost like they're nature's explorers, capable of living in places that seem completely different from one another.

Let's start with the savannahs of Africa, perhaps the most famous home of the African elephant. A savannah is a vast, open grassland dotted with trees and bushes. It's the kind of place where the sky stretches endlessly, and herds of animals, like zebras, giraffes, and antelopes, roam freely. Here, elephants move across the landscape in search of food and water, often walking dozens of miles in a single day. The savannah might look dry and dusty to us, but to an elephant, it's full of possibilities. They can eat the grass, pull leaves from trees, and even dig for water when the rivers dry up. Their strong trunks are perfect for breaking branches or reaching high into acacia trees to grab the tastiest leaves.

Water is a big deal on the savannah, and elephants are often the ones to find it first. During the dry season, when water becomes scarce, elephants remember where hidden waterholes are or use their tusks to dig wells in dry riverbeds. This doesn't just help them; it helps other animals, too. A herd of elephants drinking at a waterhole is like a gathering of all kinds of creatures—birds, monkeys, and even predators like lions come to share the water that elephants uncover.

Now, picture a dense rainforest. It's dark and humid, with towering trees and thick undergrowth. This is where you'll find some African forest elephants, a smaller and more secretive cousin of the savannah elephants. Forest elephants have shorter tusks and smaller, rounder ears, which help them navigate through the narrow paths of the jungle. Life in the forest is very different. Instead of walking long distances in open spaces, these elephants stick to trails they've carved through the trees. They munch on fruit, bark, and leaves, and as they move, they drop seeds in their dung, helping new plants grow. In many ways, they act as gardeners of the rainforest, keeping the ecosystem balanced and healthy.

Asian elephants live in forests, too, but theirs are often less dense than the rainforests of Africa. These elephants are found in countries like India, Thailand, and Sri Lanka, where they share their habitat with animals like tigers, monkeys, and deer. Unlike their African relatives, Asian elephants are more likely to be found near rivers and wetlands, where they can cool off and find food. Forests provide plenty of shade, and Asian elephants' smaller ears help them stay comfortable in these environments.

But elephants aren't just limited to forests and savannahs. Did you know that African elephants can also be found in deserts? The deserts of Namibia, for example, are home to a special group of elephants that have adapted to the harsh, dry conditions. These desert elephants are not a different species, but they've learned how to survive in one of the toughest places on Earth. They walk farther than most elephants—sometimes up to 50 miles a day—just to find food and water. They've also learned how to dig deep into the sand to uncover underground water sources. Despite the heat and lack of resources, these elephants thrive, proving just how resourceful they can be.

Swamps and wetlands are another surprising place to find elephants. In countries like Botswana, elephants gather in large numbers around the Okavango Delta, a sprawling wetland that floods seasonally. Here, elephants wade through the water, using their trunks to snorkel as they swim. They feast on water plants and drink from the many channels and pools. Watching elephants play in the water is a sight to behold—they splash, roll, and spray water with their trunks, enjoying the cool relief from the heat.

What's amazing is how elephants adapt to each of these environments. Their large bodies, strong legs, and versatile trunks allow them to find food, water, and shelter in places that might seem impossible for other animals. They know where to go and what to do, whether they're in a wide-open savannah, a tangled forest, or a harsh desert. Their ability to thrive in such different habitats shows just how intelligent and resilient they are.

But their habitats are also under threat. As humans expand cities, farms, and roads, elephants lose more and more of the places they call home. In some areas, forests are cut down for timber or farmland, leaving elephants with nowhere to go. In deserts and savannahs, water sources are sometimes diverted for human use, making it harder for elephants to survive. This is why conservation efforts are so important—to protect the habitats that elephants depend on and ensure that these incredible animals have a place to live for generations to come.

The role of elephants in their ecosystems

Elephants are often called the "gardeners of the Earth," and for a good reason. These enormous animals play a huge role in keeping their ecosystems healthy and balanced. Everything they do—from the way they eat to the paths they travel—helps other plants and animals survive. Imagine a forest or savannah as a giant puzzle, with every plant and animal being one piece. Elephants are like the piece that holds it all together. Without them, things wouldn't work the same way.

Let's start with how elephants shape their surroundings. When they move through a forest, they create trails by trampling plants and breaking branches. This might sound destructive, but it's actually very helpful. These trails act like highways for other animals, making it easier for smaller creatures to get around. Deer, monkeys, and even birds often use paths made by elephants to find food or escape predators. In a way, elephants are like nature's road builders, paving the way for everyone else.

Their eating habits also make a big difference. Elephants are herbivores, which means they eat plants, and they eat a lot of them—hundreds of pounds every day. While that might sound like they're taking more than their share, the truth is that elephants help plants grow. How? By spreading seeds. When elephants eat fruits, they don't digest the seeds inside. Instead, the seeds pass through their bodies and come out in their dung, ready to grow into new plants. Imagine eating a piece of fruit and planting the seed at the same time—that's what elephants do, but on a much bigger scale. Some trees even depend on elephants to spread their seeds. Without elephants, those trees might not grow at all.

Elephants are also amazing at finding water, which is incredibly important in dry places like savannahs and deserts. When water is hard to find, elephants use their trunks and tusks to dig wells in dry riverbeds. These wells often fill with groundwater, creating a drinkable pool not just for elephants but for other animals too. Giraffes, zebras, and even tiny birds come to these elephant-made watering holes to drink. By digging for water, elephants help entire communities of animals survive during tough times.

But it's not just other animals that benefit from elephants' actions. Plants and trees also rely on elephants in surprising ways. For example, elephants often knock over small trees or strip bark from larger ones to get to the tasty leaves or wood inside. While this might seem harmful, it actually helps prevent forests from becoming too dense. By clearing out smaller trees, elephants make room for sunlight to reach the ground, allowing grasses and smaller plants to grow. This creates a balanced ecosystem where all kinds of plants and animals can thrive.

Elephants also play an important role in nutrient cycling. When they eat and poop, they move nutrients from one part of their habitat to another. Their dung isn't just full of seeds—it's also packed with nutrients that help fertilize the soil. In fact, some plants grow better in soil that has been enriched by elephant dung. This helps entire ecosystems stay healthy and productive.

Even in death, elephants contribute to their ecosystems. When an elephant dies, its body provides food for scavengers like vultures and hyenas. Over time, the nutrients from its body return to the soil, helping plants grow. It's a reminder of how everything in nature is connected and how even the end of one life can support the beginning of others.

In wetlands and swamps, elephants have a different but equally important role. By moving through the water and pulling up plants, they keep channels open and prevent wetlands from becoming clogged with vegetation. This benefits fish, birds, and other aquatic creatures that depend on clear waterways to survive. Elephants act like caretakers, making sure these habitats stay healthy and full of life.

Elephants don't just help their immediate surroundings—they also influence the larger climate. By spreading seeds and encouraging the growth of certain plants, they contribute to the health of forests, which absorb carbon dioxide from the atmosphere. This helps combat climate change, a problem that affects the entire planet. In this way, elephants aren't just important to their local ecosystems—they're important to all of us.

2

ELEPHANT ANATOMY

Imagine an animal with a built-in tool kit. That's what elephants have! Everything about their bodies is designed to help them survive in their habitats, whether it's the dry savannah, dense forest, or even the harsh desert. Their trunks, tusks, ears, and feet aren't just interesting to look at—they're like the ultimate gadgets, each with a purpose that helps elephants live, communicate, and thrive.

Let's start with the most fascinating part of an elephant: its trunk. An elephant's trunk is not just a nose—it's also a hand, a straw, and even a trumpet. It's made up of about 40,000 muscles, which is hard to imagine when you think about how our whole body only has around 600 muscles. This incredible structure allows the trunk to bend, twist, stretch, and lift. With their trunks, elephants can pull down tree branches, pick up tiny objects like a single peanut, and even lift something as heavy as a small tree trunk. It's like having a super-strong arm that's also incredibly delicate.

Elephants also use their trunks to drink, but not the way you might think. They don't sip water directly like we do. Instead, they suck water up into their trunks—up to two gallons at a time—and then curl the trunk around to spray it into their mouths. Watching an elephant drink is like seeing a natural water pump in action. They also use their trunks to spray water over their bodies during a bath, often following it up with a coating of mud to protect their skin from the sun and bugs. It's a perfect combination of strength, precision, and practicality.

But the trunk isn't just for eating, drinking, or bathing. Elephants also use it to communicate. By making low rumbling sounds or trumpeting, they send messages to other elephants. They can even use their trunks to show affection, gently touching each other's faces or wrapping their trunks together like a hug. For baby elephants, the trunk is a toy and a learning tool. They swing it around, practice picking things up, and sometimes even trip over it. Watching a baby elephant learn to use its trunk is like watching a toddler figure out how to walk.

Now let's talk about tusks, the long, curved teeth that stick out from an elephant's face. Not all elephants have tusks, but when they do, these ivory tools are incredibly useful. Tusks are used for digging, lifting heavy objects, stripping bark off trees, and even as weapons to defend themselves. They're made of the same material as our teeth, but they keep growing throughout an elephant's life. In fact, the size of an elephant's tusks can give you clues about its age and even its habits.

Male elephants often use their tusks in battles over territory or mates. These clashes can leave marks on the tusks, which scientists study to learn more about the elephant's life. But tusks aren't just for tough jobs. Elephants also use them for delicate tasks, like gently scratching an itch or breaking open tough shells to get to the fruit inside. Unfortunately, tusks have made elephants a target for poachers, which is why so many conservation efforts focus on protecting them from harm.

Next are the ears—those massive, floppy wonders that are hard to miss. African elephants have ears shaped a bit like the continent of Africa, while Asian elephants have smaller, rounder ears. But elephant ears are more than just distinctive shapes; they're like built-in air conditioners. In hot weather, elephants flap their ears to cool down, creating a breeze that helps lower their body temperature. Inside the ears are large blood vessels, and as the air passes over them, it cools the blood, which then circulates through the elephant's body. It's a brilliant natural cooling system, especially for animals that live in such warm climates.

Ears are also a key part of an elephant's communication. By flapping their ears or holding them in certain positions, elephants can signal their mood or intentions to others in their herd. For example, wide-flared ears might mean the elephant feels threatened and is trying to look bigger to scare off a predator. In quieter moments, their ears might droop as they rest or relax. The ears are like a billboard, showing what the elephant is feeling.

Finally, we come to their feet. At first glance, elephant feet might not seem as exciting as trunks, tusks, or ears, but they're just as impressive. An elephant's foot is perfectly designed to support its massive weight. Underneath the tough skin is a spongy pad that acts like a cushion, absorbing the impact of each step. This makes elephants surprisingly quiet when they walk. Even though they can weigh as much as a small car, they can move through the forest almost silently. It's like walking on built-in shock absorbers.

Elephants are also incredibly sure-footed. Their wide, flat feet distribute their weight evenly, which helps them walk on soft, muddy ground without sinking. In deserts, their feet are just as useful, spreading out their weight to help them move across sand. And did you know elephants can actually "listen" with their feet? They can sense vibrations in the ground caused by other elephants' movements or distant sounds, almost like having an extra set of ears in their feet.

How their bodies are adapted for survival

An elephant's trunk is a superpower when it comes to eating. With more than 40,000 muscles, it's incredibly strong and flexible, allowing elephants to grab just about anything they need. Whether they're plucking tiny blades of grass or pulling down heavy branches, their trunks make it possible. They can reach up high to grab the leaves from tall trees or bend down low to pull up clumps of grass. Even tough tasks, like stripping bark off a tree, are no problem for an elephant. Their trunks act like a powerful tool and a delicate hand at the same time.

But eating isn't just about grabbing food—it's also about choosing the best bites. Elephants are picky eaters in the best way. They use the tips of their trunks, which have finger-like extensions, to feel around for the tastiest leaves and fruits. Imagine being able to sniff out a meal and pick it up with the same tool! Sometimes, elephants even shake a tree with their trunk to knock down the ripest fruit. Their ability to eat a huge variety of plants helps them stay healthy and gives them the energy they need to move around all day.

Eating as much as 300 pounds of food daily is no small task, and their trunks make it possible. But the trunk isn't just for getting food—it also helps elephants drink. You might think elephants would just lower their heads to a river or lake and sip like most animals, but that's not how it works. Instead, they use their trunks like a straw, sucking up water and then spraying it into their mouths. One trunkful can hold up to two gallons of water! It's like having a built-in water bottle that refills itself every time they find a water source.

Drinking water is essential for staying hydrated, but elephants take it a step further. On hot days, they use their trunks to spray water over their bodies, cooling themselves off and cleaning their skin. Afterward, they might toss some mud or dust on top as a kind of sunscreen and bug repellent. This not only keeps them cool but also protects their sensitive skin. Watching an elephant take a mud bath is like seeing a giant, happy kid playing in the dirt. It's practical and fun at the same time.

Beyond eating and drinking, elephants' trunks are also their main way of communicating. Just like we use our voices, elephants use their trunks to make sounds and gestures that send messages to others. Have you ever heard an elephant trumpet? That loud, trumpeting sound is made by blowing air through their trunks, and it's often a way to show excitement or warn others of danger. But trumpeting is only part of the story. Elephants also make low rumbling sounds that travel through the ground as vibrations. These sounds can be picked up by other elephants' feet, even miles away. It's like having a secret underground phone line that keeps the whole herd connected.

The trunk isn't just for making sounds—it's also a tool for showing affection and building relationships. Elephants use their trunks to touch and comfort one another, wrapping their trunks together in what looks like a hug. A mother elephant might gently guide her calf with her trunk or use it to pull the baby closer when danger is near. In herds, elephants often greet each other by touching trunks, almost like a handshake or a hug between friends. These gestures strengthen the bonds within the group, making the herd feel more like a family.

Trunks also come in handy for problem-solving, a skill elephants are famous for. If an elephant encounters an obstacle, like a fallen log blocking its path, it can use its trunk to move it out of the way. If there's a hard-to-reach piece of fruit, the trunk can grab it with ease. Elephants have even been observed using their trunks to pick up sticks or rocks and use them as tools to reach something or scratch an itch. It's a level of creativity that shows just how intelligent they are.

Baby elephants have to learn how to use their trunks, and it's not always easy. When they're born, their trunks are more like floppy noodles that they haven't quite figured out yet. You might see a baby elephant swinging its trunk around wildly or even sucking on it like a pacifier. Over time, they practice and get better, learning to pick up food, drink water, and eventually communicate with the herd. Watching a baby elephant master its trunk is like watching someone learn to ride a bike—there are a lot of wobbles and mistakes at first, but they get the hang of it eventually.

Tusks

Elephant tusks are like nature's multi-purpose tools, and for elephants, they're more than just impressive features—they're essential for survival. These long, curved teeth are made of ivory, and they grow continuously throughout an elephant's life. Whether an elephant is digging for water, stripping bark from a tree, or protecting itself and its herd, tusks are an important part of how elephants interact with the world around them.

Imagine being in a dry savannah during the peak of the dry season. Water is scarce, and most of the rivers and ponds have dried up. For many animals, this would be a serious problem. But elephants have a solution. Using their tusks, they dig deep into the ground to reach underground water sources. Their tusks are strong enough to break through hard soil, and their trunks help scoop out the loosened dirt. Soon, they've created a small, natural well that provides fresh water not just for themselves but for other animals in the area. Zebras, antelopes, and even birds come to drink from the waterholes elephants create. In this way, tusks aren't just tools for survival—they also make elephants into heroes of their ecosystem.

Tusks are also incredibly handy when it comes to finding food. Trees with thick, tough bark might seem impossible for other animals to eat, but not for elephants. They use their tusks to strip away the bark and get to the softer, more nutritious layers underneath.

This is especially important during times when food is hard to find, like in the dry season. Elephants rely on their tusks to access food that other animals can't reach, which helps them survive in harsh conditions.

But tusks aren't just for digging and scraping—they're also for breaking. If an elephant comes across a tree with fruits or leaves that are out of reach, it can use its tusks to push the tree over. This might seem like a destructive move, but it's actually part of how elephants shape their environment. By knocking over trees, they create open spaces in the forest where sunlight can reach the ground, allowing new plants to grow. Other animals, like birds and insects, take advantage of these fallen trees, using them as shelter or food sources. In this way, elephants' tusks play a role in maintaining the balance of their habitats.

Tusks are also vital for defense. While elephants are some of the largest and strongest animals on Earth, they're not entirely without enemies. Predators like lions or hyenas might target young or weak elephants, and this is where tusks come into play. Adult elephants use their tusks to fend off attackers, swinging them like weapons to protect themselves and their herd. Even a single swing of a tusk can be enough to scare off a predator. Tusks are not only tools but also a form of armor, giving elephants the upper hand in dangerous situations.

In addition to protecting themselves from predators, elephants use their tusks to compete with each other. Male elephants, especially during a period called musth

—a time when their testosterone levels are higher—often engage in battles to establish dominance or win the attention of females. These clashes can be dramatic, with elephants locking tusks and pushing against each other in displays of strength. While these fights can look intense, they're rarely fatal, and they play an important role in determining the social hierarchy of male elephants.

Not all elephants have tusks, though. While both male and female African elephants typically have tusks, only some male Asian elephants do. Female Asian elephants and tuskless males still manage just fine, relying more on their trunks and the strength of their bodies to perform tasks. In areas where poaching has been a serious problem, more tuskless elephants have been born over time, likely because tuskless elephants are less likely to be targeted by hunters. It's a reminder of how adaptable these animals are, even when faced with threats.

Tusks also hold clues about an elephant's life. Scientists study the size, shape, and wear patterns on tusks to learn about an elephant's age, diet, and even its experiences. For example, deep grooves on the tusks might show that an elephant has spent a lot of time stripping bark from trees, while a broken or worn-down tip could indicate a history of digging or fighting. Each tusk tells a story, like a natural journal of an elephant's life.

Unfortunately, tusks have also brought elephants a lot of trouble. Because tusks are made of ivory, they've been highly valued by humans for thousands of years, leading to widespread poaching. This has caused the population of elephants to decline in many parts of the world. Conservation efforts today focus on protecting elephants and stopping the illegal ivory trade. Many people are now working to ensure that elephants can keep their tusks where they belong—on the elephants themselves.

Ears

Elephants live in some of the hottest places on Earth, from the sun-baked savannahs of Africa to the steamy forests of Asia. While they're built to handle the heat, elephants don't have sweat glands like we do, so they can't just cool off by sweating. Instead, they rely on their massive, flappy ears as a unique and effective cooling system. Their ears are more than just big and noticeable—they're a crucial adaptation that helps elephants keep their body temperature under control and survive in challenging climates.

If you've ever seen an elephant in the wild or on TV, you may have noticed how often they flap their ears. It might look like they're just waving away flies or making funny faces, but what they're really doing is cooling themselves down. Elephants' ears are packed with blood vessels, especially close to the surface of the skin. By flapping their ears, elephants create a breeze that cools the blood flowing through these vessels. Once this cooler blood circulates back into the rest of their body, it helps lower their overall temperature, almost like a natural air conditioning system.

The size of their ears also makes a big difference. African elephants have much larger ears than Asian elephants, which makes sense when you think about where they live. African elephants roam across open savannahs and dry deserts where temperatures can soar, sometimes reaching over 100 degrees Fahrenheit. Their big ears, shaped somewhat like the continent of Africa, provide a large surface area for cooling. Asian elephants, on the other hand, live in forests and jungles where it's often humid but shaded. They don't need as much cooling power, so their ears are smaller and rounder. This difference in ear size is a great example of how elephants have adapted to suit their specific environments.

Flapping isn't the only way elephants use their ears to cool down. Sometimes, they'll hold their ears out to the side, creating more airflow across their skin. It's almost like they're holding up giant fans on either side of their heads, catching as much breeze as possible. This is especially useful when they're standing still or resting in the shade. By simply adjusting the position of their ears, they can control how much heat they lose, which is pretty amazing when you think about it.

Beyond just keeping themselves cool, elephants' ears help them stay comfortable and alert. They can move their ears in different directions, like built-in radar dishes, to pick up sounds from all around them. Elephants have excellent hearing, and their large ears help them detect even faint noises over long distances. This ability to listen closely is especially helpful in the wild, where they need to be aware of potential threats, like predators or nearby humans. By listening carefully, elephants can sense when danger is approaching and decide whether to move away or stay put.

Elephants also use their ears to communicate with each other. When an elephant is calm, its ears may rest loosely by its sides. But if it feels threatened, it might flare its ears out to make itself look larger and more intimidating. This ear display can be a warning to predators or even to other elephants, signaling that it's ready to defend itself or its family. In a way, elephants' ears are like body language, showing how they feel and what they're about to do.

Because of the importance of their ears, elephants take good care of them. You'll often see elephants flicking their ears to shake off dust or rubbing them against trees to scratch an itch. Sometimes, when they're near water, they'll use their trunks to spray water over their ears, cooling them down even faster. This mix of flapping, spraying, and positioning helps elephants manage the heat and stay comfortable in their environment.

Young elephants learn from older elephants how to use their ears effectively. Baby elephants start flapping their ears early on, but it takes time for them to fully understand how to use them for cooling and communication. Watching young elephants grow and experiment with their ears is like seeing a child learn to express themselves—they're figuring out how to use their body language to connect with others and adapt to their surroundings.

An elephant's ears also play a role in the health of the herd. In the wild, herds often travel long distances to find food and water, especially during the dry season. Large ears help elephants stay cooler during these journeys, reducing the risk of overheating. When one elephant senses a water source, it might flap its ears excitedly, alerting the others to follow. This "ear language" is part of the social communication that keeps the herd together and safe.

Incredible memory and brainpower

Elephants have been called "the animals that never forget," and there's truth to that. Their powerful memory helps them remember important details, like where to find water during dry seasons or which paths are safe to take. Imagine being able to remember exactly where a waterhole is located, even if you haven't visited it for years. Elephants can do this, which is crucial for their survival. In the dry landscapes of Africa or Asia, a reliable memory can mean the difference between life and death.

This memory isn't just useful for finding water; it's

also essential for navigating their world. Elephants remember their migration routes, which can stretch across hundreds of miles. These routes aren't marked by signs or maps, but by memories passed down through generations. The matriarch, or the oldest female in the herd, often leads the group. She's like a walking encyclopedia, filled with knowledge about food sources, waterholes, and places to avoid. Her memory helps keep the whole herd safe, and younger elephants learn from her as they travel together.

Elephants are also skilled at recognizing faces. Studies have shown that elephants can recognize hundreds of different faces, not only of other elephants but also of humans. This ability to remember faces helps them distinguish between friend and foe. In areas where elephants are protected and treated kindly, they become familiar with the people around them and often feel safe. But in places where they've faced threats from humans, elephants remember specific individuals who have harmed them or their herd, and they react cautiously around them.

One amazing example of an elephant's memory involves elephants remembering other elephants they've bonded with, even if they've been separated for years. Imagine two elephants who grew up together in the same herd but were later separated due to natural events or human intervention. Decades might pass, but if they meet again, they'll often show signs of recognition and joy. They might trumpet, flap their ears, or intertwine their trunks in what looks like an elephant hug. This ability to remember other elephants for such a long time speaks to the depth of their memory and the strength of their social bonds.

Elephants also have a complex way of understanding emotions, both in themselves and in others. If an elephant in the herd passes away, the other elephants often show behaviors that look a lot like mourning. They might stand around the body, gently touching it with their trunks, as if saying goodbye. Even years after an elephant has died, its relatives might return to the spot and pause, as though they're remembering the one they lost. This kind of behavior is extremely rare in the animal kingdom and is another example of the unique emotional depth and memory of elephants.

The incredible brainpower of elephants doesn't stop at memory—they're also great problem-solvers. In the wild, elephants are known to use tools, like picking up sticks or branches with their trunks to swat away flies or scratch an itch in hard-to-reach places. They've been observed using leaves or bark to cover muddy areas, creating a path for other elephants to walk on without sinking. This kind of creativity is similar to what you'd see in primates, like chimpanzees, and shows just how adaptable and intelligent elephants can be.

Their problem-solving skills are also apparent in their interactions with humans. In some parts of Africa, farmers have struggled with elephants eating their crops. But when they tried using bees to keep the elephants away—since elephants don't like the sound of buzzing—the elephants quickly learned to avoid those areas. In response, farmers have started using beehive fences to protect their crops, which has helped reduce conflict between people and elephants. The elephants' ability to learn and adapt to this new situation highlights just how quickly they can pick up on new information and change their behavior.

Elephants also learn from each other, especially from older, more experienced members of the herd. This social learning is essential for young elephants, who need to understand where to find food, how to use their trunks, and what dangers to avoid. Older elephants, particularly the matriarch, pass down knowledge through example, guiding the younger members as they move through their territory. This transfer of knowledge is similar to how humans teach their children, making elephants one of the few animals with a culture that includes learning and teaching.

Another area where elephants show their intelligence is in their communication. Elephants use a wide range of vocalizations, from trumpets to rumbles, to share information with each other. Some of these sounds are so low-pitched that humans can't hear them, but they travel through the ground as vibrations. Other elephants can sense these vibrations through their feet, even from miles away. This form of long-distance communication allows elephants to keep in touch, even if they're far apart. It's like having a built-in messaging system, allowing them to coordinate their movements and warn each other about dangers.

The complexity of their brains allows elephants to form bonds that are as meaningful as friendships. In their herds, elephants form close connections with certain individuals, spending more time with them, playing, and even showing affection through trunk touches and gentle nudges. These friendships add to the overall stability and happiness of the herd. Elephants have even been known to help each other when one is in trouble. If a young elephant gets stuck in mud, the adults will work together to pull it out using their trunks and tusks. This cooperative behavior is not only a sign of their intelligence but also of their strong social structure.

Elephants' brains also help them experience and express emotions that are similar to our own. They feel joy, grief, curiosity, and even empathy. If one elephant is hurt or distressed, others in the herd may gather around, gently touching it with their trunks as if offering comfort. This empathy makes elephants one of the most emotionally complex animals on the planet, and it's part of what makes them so fascinating to humans.

3

ELEPHANT FAMILY LIFE

In most elephant herds, the matriarch is the oldest and most experienced female. She's the one who guides the herd, using her knowledge of where to find food, water, and safe paths to travel. Her leadership isn't based on size or strength, but on wisdom. Because elephants have such incredible memories, the matriarch remembers important details that can mean the difference between life and death for her family. She knows the landscape, recalls locations of hidden waterholes, remembers which areas are dangerous, and is familiar with the routes the herd has taken over the years.

The matriarch isn't just a guide—she's a teacher. Younger elephants learn by watching her and following her example. When the herd encounters something new or challenging, the matriarch is often the first to react, showing the others what to do. For instance, if the herd comes across a river, the matriarch will choose the safest place to cross and lead the way, often testing the depth of the water with her trunk before allowing the others to follow. By observing her, young elephants learn the skills they'll need as they grow older, and when the matriarch eventually passes away, another experienced female in the herd will take her place, continuing this cycle of learning and leadership.

Life in an elephant herd revolves around this close family bond. Elephants don't live alone; they thrive in groups that feel more like big, extended families. Most herds are made up of the matriarch, her daughters, and their young. Sons stay with the herd until they're teenagers, but as they mature, they often leave to join groups of other males or to live more solitary lives. This structure means that female elephants spend their entire lives together, building incredibly strong relationships that last for decades. Each member of the herd has a role to play, whether it's protecting the calves, finding food, or keeping an eye out for danger.

Communication is key to keeping the herd connected, and elephants have developed many ways to stay in touch. They use low rumbles that can travel for miles through the ground, allowing them to "speak" to each other even when they're far apart. By sensing these vibrations through their feet, elephants can keep track of where everyone is, whether they're nearby or separated by great distances. This long-distance communication is especially important when the herd is on the move, helping them stay together even as they navigate vast landscapes.

The herd doesn't just rely on the matriarch's knowledge; they also lean on each other emotionally. When a young calf is born, the entire herd becomes its support system. Mothers, aunts, sisters, and cousins all take part in helping to care for the newborn. If a mother needs to rest or find food, another female might babysit the calf, making sure it's safe and comfortable. These "alloparents" (or helper mothers) play a crucial role in raising young elephants, sharing the responsibility of caring for and protecting them. This support system allows mothers to recover their strength and ensures that calves grow up surrounded by love and protection.

Baby elephants are born into this nurturing environment and learn from day one what it means to be part of the herd. They quickly become the center of attention, and it's not uncommon to see other elephants crowding around, reaching out with their trunks to touch and welcome the newborn. The entire herd is invested in the calf's survival, and this sense of shared responsibility creates an environment where young elephants feel safe and secure as they grow and learn.

Elephants are also known for showing empathy toward each other, especially during tough times. If an elephant is injured or sick, the herd doesn't just leave it behind. Instead, they will often stay close, offering support in the form of gentle touches with their trunks and staying nearby to provide comfort. They've even been observed bringing food and water to injured members. This compassionate behavior strengthens their bonds and ensures that each member of the herd knows they're part of a group that cares for one another.

The herd's strong social bonds are evident during moments of loss as well. If an elephant in the herd dies, the others show behaviors that look a lot like mourning. They might stand around the body, touching it with their trunks and staying close for hours or even days. Sometimes, elephants will revisit the place where a loved one passed away, pausing as if to pay their respects. These acts of remembrance show that elephants don't just live together—they form deep emotional connections that last a lifetime.

Living in a herd also helps elephants defend against predators. While adult elephants don't have many natural enemies due to their size and strength, young calves are vulnerable to attacks from predators like lions or hyenas. In these situations, the herd comes together to protect their young. They form a circle around the calves, with the adults facing outward and their trunks raised, ready to defend the herd if necessary. This instinctive behavior creates a strong line of defense that keeps the calves safe from harm.

Male elephants, as they mature, often leave the herd to join groups of other males or live alone. However, they don't lose their connection to the herd entirely. They might return occasionally, especially during mating season, or they may travel alongside other herds when food and water are plentiful. These bachelor groups allow young males to socialize, practice sparring, and learn from each other. While they don't have the same close-knit relationships as females within the herd, they still benefit from the social learning that these groups provide.

Each member of the herd, from the youngest calf to the experienced matriarch, has a role that contributes to the group's survival and happiness. Life in a herd teaches elephants about loyalty, responsibility, and care. They support each other in ways that remind us of human families, sharing not just resources but also knowledge, affection, and protection.

Baby elephants

At birth, a baby elephant is about three feet tall and weighs around 200 pounds. That might sound big, but compared to the adults towering over it, the calf seems tiny. It's covered in a fine layer of fuzz, its trunk flops around as it figures out how to control it, and it clings close to its mother, seeking her warmth and protection. Within a few hours, though, the calf is standing on its own shaky legs, taking its first clumsy steps. And while those first steps may be wobbly, they mark the beginning of a journey that will be guided by the love and support of its entire herd.

Life for a baby elephant is all about learning, exploring, and bonding with its family. In the early weeks, the calf rarely strays far from its mother. She is its main source of nourishment, as it drinks her milk to gain strength. Just like a human baby, a calf relies completely on its mother for food, comfort, and safety. It uses her as a constant anchor, staying so close that its small body is often hidden behind her large legs. If the calf becomes frightened, it might even walk underneath its mother's belly, using her as a kind of "shelter" against any unfamiliar sights or sounds.

As the calf grows, it begins to take in the world around it with wide-eyed curiosity. Everything is new and exciting, from the trees and grass to the other animals wandering nearby. Calves are naturally playful, and they quickly start interacting with the other young elephants in the herd. They chase each other around, gently bump into each other, and experiment with their trunks. Just like human toddlers, they're clumsy, curious, and always learning through play. Sometimes, they try to copy the actions of the older elephants, like attempting to lift small branches with their trunks or splashing around in waterholes. Watching a baby elephant discover these things for the first time is both funny and heartwarming.

The trunk, in particular, is a source of fascination for a young elephant. At first, it doesn't quite know how to use it. The trunk seems to have a mind of its own, swinging around uncontrollably or getting tangled up in everything. Sometimes, calves even suck on their trunks for comfort, just like a human baby might suck its thumb. Over time, and with plenty of practice, the calf learns how to control its trunk, using it to explore the ground, pick up food, and drink water. This process takes years, but the other members of the herd are patient teachers, showing the calf different ways to use its trunk for all kinds of tasks.

In a herd, a calf is never alone. Other females in the group, including aunts and older sisters, often act as "alloparents" or babysitters. These family members help take care of the calf, providing a watchful eye when the mother needs to rest or find food. This support allows the calf to feel secure and gives the mother a chance to recover her energy. The herd as a whole shares in the responsibility of raising each calf, which strengthens their bonds and makes the herd feel like one big family. For the calf, this means that there's always someone nearby to lean on, to play with, or to learn from.

Waterholes are especially exciting places for young elephants. When the herd reaches one, the calves eagerly follow the adults into the water, often tripping over their own legs in the rush to get in. Once there, they splash, roll, and play, sometimes squirting water from their trunks and trying to copy the adults. Mud baths are just as fun, as the calves learn to roll around in the mud, coating their skin to keep cool and protect against insects. These playful moments are not only fun; they're also important lessons in survival. Learning how to keep cool and protect their skin is a skill they'll need for the rest of their lives.

The calf's world is filled with sounds that help it learn about its family and surroundings. Elephants communicate with a wide range of rumbles, trumpets, and low-frequency calls. Calves listen carefully to these sounds, learning what each one means and how to respond. They quickly learn to recognize their mother's voice, as well as the voices of other close relatives. As they grow older, they start to experiment with their own vocalizations, trying to mimic the sounds of the adults. Each call has its purpose, whether it's calling the herd together, signaling danger, or simply greeting a family member. This "language" is part of how the calf begins to understand its place in the family and the world around it.

Challenges are part of every calf's journey, and learning to navigate the wild is no small feat. As the calf grows, it's introduced to the daily challenges of finding food and water, avoiding danger, and keeping up with the herd. If there's a predator nearby, the herd will gather around the calves, forming a protective barrier of adult bodies to keep them safe. During these moments, the calf learns to trust in the strength of the herd, understanding that it's part of a family that will always look out for it. These early lessons teach the calf about loyalty, safety, and the importance of sticking together.

Over time, as the calf grows stronger and more confident, it begins to explore more independently. While it will still stay close to the herd, it may wander a little farther or try more complex tasks, like pulling leaves from branches or splashing alone at the waterhole. With each new experience, the calf becomes more skilled and self-assured, preparing for a future where it will play a larger role within the family group.

Roles of males and females in elephant society

Female elephants are the heart and soul of the herd. They live in matriarch-led groups, which means that the oldest and most experienced female is in charge. She's known as the matriarch, and her wisdom is invaluable. She leads the herd, makes important decisions, and teaches the younger elephants everything they need to know. Female elephants stay in these herds for their entire lives, forming strong bonds with their mothers, sisters, aunts, and daughters. These relationships create a stable, loving environment where knowledge is passed down from one generation to the next. Every female plays a role, from protecting the young to helping find food and water.

Life in a female-led herd is a constant collaboration. Each female has a part to play, and they all support one another, especially in caring for calves. Older females act as babysitters for the young ones, watching over them while their mothers graze or rest. This cooperation helps everyone in the herd. The calves get the attention and protection they need, and the mothers have time to regain their strength. This shared responsibility also deepens the bonds between the females, making them a strong and united family.

The matriarch, as the leader, is the most trusted member of the herd. Her experience is what guides them, especially during challenging times like droughts, when food and water are hard to find. She remembers where to find hidden waterholes and which paths are safe. Her role is not just about strength—it's about wisdom, patience, and guidance. The matriarch teaches by example, showing younger elephants how to survive and care for each other. When the matriarch eventually grows too old to lead, another experienced female, usually her oldest daughter, will take over. This passing of leadership keeps the herd strong and ensures that the wisdom of the matriarch is never lost.

While females stay close to their families, male elephants lead a very different life. When male elephants, or bulls, reach adolescence—usually around the age of 12 to 15—they start to feel the urge to leave the herd. This isn't because they don't care about their family; it's simply the natural course of life for male elephants. Bulls leave the herd to either live alone or join a group of other males, known as a bachelor herd. These bachelor groups are more loosely bonded than family herds, but they still provide companionship and learning opportunities for younger males.

Life for a male elephant outside the family herd is full of new challenges and responsibilities. Without the daily protection and guidance of the matriarch and the herd, young bulls have to learn how to find food and water on their own. This independence helps them grow stronger and more self-reliant. Older bulls in a bachelor herd often serve as mentors for younger males, teaching them how to survive and preparing them for encounters with other bulls. These lessons are crucial because male elephants eventually enter a period called musth, a time when their hormone levels increase dramatically. During musth, bulls become more aggressive and competitive as they seek out mates, and they need the strength and experience to handle this intense period.

Musth is an important phase for male elephants, as it's their time to prove themselves and establish dominance. When a bull is in musth, he will sometimes challenge other males in contests of strength to win the attention of females. These challenges are often more about showing power than causing harm, as most bulls try to avoid serious injuries. Through these displays of strength, bulls establish a social order among themselves. Older, more experienced bulls usually dominate, but younger males learn from these encounters, gaining the skills and confidence they'll need as they mature.

Even though male and female elephants live mostly separate lives, they do come together during mating season. Bulls seek out herds and approach females, displaying behaviors to show their interest. During this time, the bonds between males and females are renewed, if only briefly, before the males continue on their independent paths. Once mating is over, the bull will move on, and the female returns to her herd, where she'll be supported by her family during her long pregnancy.

Male elephants may live away from the family herd, but they still share a connection with it. Bulls often return to visit their family from time to time, especially when they're not in musth. These visits provide a chance for the younger calves and female elephants to reunite with their male relatives, reminding everyone of their shared bonds. Bulls don't lose their family ties entirely; they simply live differently, balancing independence with occasional visits to their original herd.

In elephant society, the roles of males and females complement each other beautifully. Female elephants create stability, wisdom, and support within the herd, passing down knowledge and caring for each other as they move through life together. Male elephants, on the other hand, bring strength and diversity to the gene pool, challenging themselves to grow and adapt as they move independently through the world. This balance keeps the elephant population healthy, ensuring that both males and females contribute in ways that are essential for the survival and success of the species.

Communication

One of the most powerful and well-known sounds elephants make is trumpeting. You've probably heard it before in a movie or a nature documentary—an ear-splitting, triumphant blast that seems to fill the air.

Trumpeting is the sound elephants use to express intense emotions. It's often a call of excitement, joy, or alarm. Imagine a young calf seeing its older sibling after they've been separated for a while. It might let out a short, happy trumpet as it rushes over. Or picture a group of elephants finding a waterhole after a long, hot walk. The excitement of fresh water can lead to trumpeting as they greet each other around the pool.

Trumpeting can also signal danger or alert the herd to something unusual. If a predator, like a lion, comes too close to the herd, one of the adults might trumpet loudly to signal a warning. This trumpet is sharper and louder, designed to startle the predator and communicate urgency to the other elephants. In an instant, the herd gathers, with the adults surrounding the calves to form a protective barrier. The trumpeting isn't just noise —it's a call to action, urging the herd to prepare and stay vigilant.

While trumpeting is an attention-grabber, elephants also communicate in softer, deeper tones called rumbles. These rumbles are fascinating because they travel long distances, allowing elephants to "talk" to each other even when they're far apart. The sound waves from these rumbles move through the ground as vibrations, and other elephants can pick up these signals through their feet. It's like sending a message through the earth itself. Elephants have sensitive nerve endings in their feet and trunks that can detect these low-frequency vibrations. By feeling these rumbles, they stay connected to each other, even when they're miles away.

Rumbles can mean many things, from a simple "I'm here" to more complex messages. A mother elephant might rumble softly to let her calf know where she is, especially if the calf is wandering nearby. Rumbles also help keep the herd together during migrations, which can cover vast areas. As they travel, elephants send and receive these low, comforting sounds, reassuring each other and confirming that everyone is safe and on the right path. It's an amazing system of long-distance communication that relies on their unique ability to sense sound through the earth.

Body language is another key part of how elephants communicate. Every part of their body—from their ears to their trunk—can be used to send a message. For example, when an elephant flares its ears and raises its head high, it's showing dominance or trying to appear larger and more intimidating. This is often a sign of aggression, warning others to back off. On the other hand, when elephants fold their ears back and lower their heads, they're displaying submission or calmness. By adjusting their body posture, elephants can communicate how they feel and what they're about to do, even without making a sound.

Their trunks, in particular, are incredibly expressive. Elephants use their trunks to show affection, curiosity, and concern. When two elephants meet, they might wrap their trunks together in a greeting that's almost like a handshake. Calves use their trunks to reach out to their mothers, seeking reassurance or comfort. If an elephant is hurt or distressed, others in the herd might gently touch it with their trunks, offering comfort and support. This gentle touch is a way of saying, "I'm here for you." It's heartwarming to see such a strong, powerful animal use its trunk with such tenderness.

Elephants also use their trunks to play, especially the younger ones. Calves often poke, prod, and swing their trunks at each other during playtime. These interactions not only strengthen their trunks but also teach them social skills. Play is an important part of growing up, and through these playful trunk gestures, calves learn boundaries and the social cues that are important in elephant society. The older elephants watch over them, occasionally stepping in if the play gets too rough, but mostly letting them explore and learn.

Ears, too, have a language of their own. When elephants are alert or curious, they might spread their ears wide to catch more sound and make themselves look bigger. This is useful for checking out new surroundings or facing a potential threat. In relaxed moments, like when they're grazing or resting, their ears often hang loosely by their sides. The position and movement of an elephant's ears can reveal a lot about its mood and intentions, helping the herd understand each other's emotions and reactions.

Tail movements also play a part in elephant communication. A relaxed, swishing tail shows that an elephant feels calm and content. But if its tail is raised or held stiffly, it could signal excitement, fear, or even aggression. This body language acts as a signal to the rest of the herd, letting them know whether everything is fine or if there's something they need to pay attention to. These subtle cues help the herd stay in sync, even when there's no immediate danger.

Elephants also display unique behaviors when they're grieving, showing the depth of their emotional intelligence. If an elephant passes away, the herd often gathers around, touching the body with their trunks and standing silently together. This moment of togetherness helps them acknowledge the loss and comfort each other. Elephants have even been known to visit the bones of their deceased, gently touching them and standing quietly, as if remembering their lost friend or family member. These actions show how important communication and connection are in their lives, even during moments of sadness.

Another fascinating aspect of elephant communication is how they recognize each other's voices. Each elephant has a unique sound, much like our voices are distinct. When two elephants meet after a long time apart, they might rumble or trumpet in excitement, recognizing each other's individual call. This ability to remember each other's sounds is essential for family groups that sometimes separate and reunite over long distances. Their voices become part of their identity, a unique "name" that helps them stay connected in their complex social world.

4

WHAT ELEPHANTS EAT

Elephants have big appetites, and with good reason—these enormous animals need a lot of fuel to keep going! As herbivores, they don't eat meat but instead rely on a diet of plants, fruits, bark, and other vegetation. In the wild, an adult elephant can eat up to 300 pounds of food every day. Just imagine that! It's like eating hundreds of salads, bowls of fruit, and even tree bark all in a single day. Their diet plays a huge role in shaping the landscapes around them, turning elephants into both powerful eaters and important caretakers of their environment.

Grass is a staple in an elephant's diet, especially for African elephants who roam the wide-open savannahs. As they move through the grasslands, they munch on tall grasses, pulling them up with their trunks and stripping the blades before chewing them. Grass is easy to find and grows back quickly, so it's a perfect food source for elephants. They can spend hours grazing, slowly working their way across fields as they eat. For an elephant, grazing isn't just about filling up—it's also a social activity. Often, the herd moves together as they eat, stopping and starting in sync with each other, sharing the experience of their meal.

But grass alone wouldn't be enough for such a big animal. To stay healthy, elephants also seek out other plants, like leaves, flowers, and even small shrubs. Their trunks are perfect for picking leaves off trees or pulling down branches to get at the tastiest bits. Different plants offer different nutrients, so by eating a variety of vegetation, elephants get a balanced diet that keeps them strong and energetic. As they reach up high for leaves or strip branches clean, they sometimes knock over small trees or clear dense vegetation. This might seem destructive, but it's actually helpful for the ecosystem. By opening up space and letting sunlight reach the ground, elephants create room for new plants to grow, which benefits other animals too.

Fruits are another treat elephants enjoy, though they aren't always easy to find. When the right season comes, elephants seek out fruiting trees, like marula and fig trees, and use their trunks to pluck the fruits. Imagine a giant with a sweet tooth—that's an elephant when it finds a tree loaded with ripe, juicy fruit. They can smell the fruit from far away, and they'll travel long distances just to reach a tree heavy with treats. Once they find it, the entire herd might gather around, eagerly plucking fruits and sharing the bounty. Fruits give elephants a burst of natural sugars, which boosts their energy, and also provide important vitamins.

Bark is an unusual part of an elephant's diet, but it's surprisingly nutritious. Beneath the tough outer layer of tree bark is a softer, nutrient-rich layer called cambium, which provides essential minerals. Elephants use their strong tusks to strip the bark off trees, revealing the cambium underneath. With their trunks, they peel away the strips and eat them, getting nutrients that aren't available in other parts of their diet. Stripping bark is a skill that young elephants learn by watching adults, who are careful not to strip too much bark from one tree. This way, they can return to the tree later when it has had time to recover.

Elephants also have a taste for roots, especially during the dry season when food is scarce. Using their trunks and tusks, they dig into the ground to pull up roots, which are often packed with water and nutrients. In deserts, where water is especially precious, roots are an essential part of an elephant's diet because they help them stay hydrated. Digging for roots can be hard work, but it's worth it. The roots are full of moisture, and they're often one of the few reliable food sources in harsh environments. Elephants are patient and determined when it comes to digging, using their trunks like shovels and their tusks as tools to pry roots from the earth.

The diet of Asian elephants is a bit different from

that of African elephants, mainly because they live in forests and jungles rather than open savannahs. Asian elephants eat a lot of bamboo, which grows quickly and provides plenty of fiber. They also enjoy bananas, jackfruit, and other tropical fruits that grow in their native habitats. In the dense forests of Asia, there are more trees and fewer grasses, so Asian elephants rely on a larger variety of leaves, vines, and bark. Their smaller, more nimble trunks are ideal for carefully picking through branches and leaves, allowing them to reach food in thick, tangled vegetation.

Water is another essential part of an elephant's diet, though they don't exactly "eat" it. With their large size and active lifestyle, elephants need to drink a lot of water —up to 50 gallons each day! When they find a waterhole, they drink deeply, using their trunks to draw up water and then spray it into their mouths. Waterholes also serve as social spots, where elephants from different herds sometimes meet, drink, and interact. After a long drink, elephants often cool off by splashing water over themselves or taking a mud bath, which helps protect their skin from the sun and keeps insects away.

Every part of an elephant's diet—whether it's grass, leaves, fruit, bark, roots, or water—contributes to the health of their ecosystem. As they move, eat, and drink, elephants spread seeds through their dung, creating new growth wherever they go. Their dung is full of seeds from the fruits and plants they consume, and when it lands on the ground, it acts as a natural fertilizer, helping new plants grow. This process is called seed dispersal, and it's one of the ways elephants support their environment. By spreading seeds and making room for new growth, elephants help keep their habitats diverse and thriving.

An elephant's diet might seem simple, but it's actually a complex mix that changes with the seasons and the landscape. They are incredibly adaptable eaters, adjusting their habits based on what's available and where they are. This adaptability is part of what makes them successful in such a wide range of environments, from lush forests to dry savannahs and even deserts. Each type of food offers something unique, whether it's the energy from fruit, the nutrients from bark, or the moisture from roots, and by combining these foods, elephants get everything they need to stay healthy and strong.

How much an elephant eats in a day

Elephants are famous for their enormous appetites, and it's no surprise—keeping a body that size moving takes a lot of energy! Every day, an adult elephant can eat up to 300 pounds of food. That's like eating the weight of three grown humans in leaves, grass, bark, and fruits every single day. Imagine if you had to eat that much food! The amount an elephant eats depends on the season, what's available, and the individual elephant's size, but they're always on the lookout for their next meal.

For elephants, eating isn't just a meal but an all-day activity. They spend up to 16 hours a day foraging and grazing. While some animals might take a break after a meal, elephants are nearly always munching on something. They move from spot to spot, using their trunks to grab grasses, pluck leaves, and strip bark. It's a slow process—imagine pulling up blades of grass one by one with your hand—but elephants are incredibly efficient, and their trunks are perfect for the job.

Grass is one of the main things elephants eat, especially in open savannahs where it's easy to find. An elephant might pull up clumps of grass with its trunk, shake off the dirt, and then stuff it into its mouth. They can eat hundreds of pounds of grass in a single day! While grass is filling, it's not the most nutritious food, which is why elephants also look for other foods to balance their diet.

Elephants have a bit of a sweet tooth and enjoy snacking on fruits whenever they can find them. A single elephant can eat hundreds of fruits in a day, especially when they find a tree full of ripe treats like marula or figs. Fruits provide a quick burst of energy, along with vitamins and minerals that help keep elephants healthy. When fruit is in season, an elephant herd might travel miles just to reach a tree that's full of fresh, juicy snacks. But fruits alone wouldn't keep them going all day, which is why they keep moving and sampling whatever vegetation they come across.

Leaves and branches are another major part of an

elephant's diet, and they offer important nutrients that elephants need. Elephants often reach up into the trees with their trunks to grab the tastiest leaves, sometimes using their strength to pull down entire branches. If a branch is too thick or high up, they might even push the tree over to get what they want. Stripping leaves from trees can take time, but it provides essential fiber and minerals that keep elephants healthy and strong. By moving through different parts of the landscape and sampling a variety of leaves, elephants get a range of nutrients from different plants.

Bark might not sound very tasty to us, but for elephants, it's a crucial part of their diet. Beneath the rough outer layer of bark lies the cambium, a softer, nutrient-rich layer that's packed with minerals. Using their tusks and trunks, elephants strip the bark off trees to get to this hidden treasure. Bark-eating takes patience and skill, and younger elephants often watch the adults to learn how to do it. This rich food source helps them stay nourished, especially when other foods are scarce.

Roots are another treat that elephants dig up, especially during dry seasons. Digging for roots can be hard work, but it's worth the effort. Roots are packed with water, and they're one of the few food sources that stay underground, even when other plants dry up. Using their trunks and tusks like shovels, elephants can pull up roots from deep below the ground, giving them a tasty, hydrating snack. This digging also loosens the soil, allowing new plants to grow, which benefits the entire ecosystem.

Given how much they eat, elephants are constantly on the move. They can't stay in one place for too long because they would quickly consume all the food available. Instead, they roam over large areas, sometimes covering dozens of miles in a single day. This movement not only helps them find food but also benefits the land. As elephants travel and eat, they spread seeds in their dung, which acts as a natural fertilizer. This process helps new plants grow, ensuring that there's always something for the herd to eat when they return to the area later.

Water is essential too, especially in dry, hot climates. Elephants need up to 50 gallons of water each day, and when they find a waterhole, they don't just drink—they'll often splash around, cooling off and playing in the water. Waterholes are gathering places for elephants, where they can drink their fill and socialize with others. During dry seasons, elephants use their keen memory to remember where hidden water sources are, sometimes digging with their trunks to access underground water. This natural ability to find and create water sources helps them survive, even when conditions are tough.

When young elephants are still nursing, they rely on their mothers for milk, which provides all the nutrients they need. As they get older, they begin to explore solid foods, experimenting with leaves and grass under the watchful eyes of their family. Learning to eat like an adult takes time, and young elephants practice picking up food with their trunks and chewing tough leaves and bark. It's a gradual process, and the older members of the herd are there to guide and support them as they make the transition to a full-grown diet.

The daily quest for food and water keeps elephants busy, but it also shapes their environment in powerful ways. As they consume such vast amounts, elephants help manage vegetation, keeping plant life from growing too dense in one area. They create clearings in forests, spread seeds, and even provide food for other animals that rely on the plants that elephants leave behind. Their eating habits play a key role in maintaining the health of their ecosystems, making them essential to the balance of nature.

Elephants as gardeners of the forest

Elephants are more than just big eaters—they're like nature's gardeners, shaping their environment with every mouthful. As they move through forests and savannahs, eating leaves, stripping bark, digging for roots, and spreading seeds, they leave behind changes that impact the land and help other plants and animals thrive. In a way, elephants aren't just part of their habitat; they help create it, transforming landscapes in ways that allow life to flourish.

Imagine a dense forest where sunlight barely touches the ground. For many plants, light is essential for growth, but in a crowded forest, there isn't much space for new plants to reach the sun. This is where elephants come in. As they feed on trees and bushes, they clear away branches and even knock over small trees, creating open spaces in the canopy. Sunlight pours into these gaps, allowing grasses, shrubs, and smaller trees to grow. These new plants provide food and shelter for animals like birds, insects, and small mammals. Without elephants, the forest floor might stay too dark for many plants to grow, leaving fewer resources for other creatures.

In addition to clearing space, elephants help with another important task: spreading seeds. When they eat fruits, the seeds inside don't get digested; instead, they pass through the elephant's body and end up in the ground as part of their dung. This natural fertilizer is packed with nutrients, providing a rich environment for seeds to sprout and grow. It's like planting a garden with built-in plant food! Some plants even rely on elephants to spread their seeds, as other animals either can't eat the tough fruit or can't travel as far. As elephants wander across miles of land, they drop seeds along the way, creating new growth wherever they go. Over time, this seed-spreading process leads to new trees, bushes, and grasses, adding diversity to the landscape.

Elephants also impact water sources, which are essential for life in the wild. During dry seasons, they dig into riverbeds and soil to reach underground water, creating small wells that other animals rely on. By using their tusks and trunks to dig, elephants reveal fresh water that birds, antelope, and even predators like lions come to drink. These waterholes are lifesavers in arid areas, helping all kinds of animals survive when rivers and lakes dry up. Elephants' actions make them like caretakers of the land, ensuring that other creatures have what they need to live.

Their eating habits can have a big impact on the types of plants that grow in an area. For example, elephants enjoy eating certain trees, like the acacia tree, which has sharp thorns and tough bark. By eating these trees and preventing them from growing too densely, elephants allow other plants, like grasses and small shrubs, to flourish. This creates a more balanced landscape where a variety of plants can thrive, supporting a wide range of herbivores, from zebras to gazelles. In areas without elephants, certain types of plants might grow out of control, crowding out other species and reducing biodiversity. By choosing what to eat and where to graze, elephants help keep plant life balanced and diverse.

Even their heavy footsteps play a role in shaping the environment. As elephants move, their large feet press into the soil, creating shallow depressions that collect rainwater. These small puddles provide drinking water for insects, frogs, and birds, and they also help seeds germinate by providing moisture in dry areas. Over time, elephant trails become natural paths through the forest or savannah, making it easier for other animals to navigate the landscape. These trails lead to water sources, feeding grounds, and shelter, creating a network of pathways that benefit the entire ecosystem.

Elephants' habit of pushing down trees might look destructive at first, but it actually helps create a mosaic of different habitats. In forests, the fallen trees create open patches where sunlight reaches the ground, while in savannahs, the open spaces created by fallen trees allow grasses to grow. This mix of open areas and dense vegetation provides a variety of habitats for different species, from birds that nest in the trees to small animals that hide in the underbrush. By creating these different spaces, elephants support a rich diversity of life, making room for everything from beetles to big cats.

Younger elephants learn how to "garden" from the older ones, watching as they strip bark, dig for roots, and sample leaves from different plants. This behavior isn't random; older elephants know which plants are best to eat and how to get to hidden sources of food and water. Young elephants copy these actions, learning which plants are edible, which trees to avoid, and where to find the best food. This shared knowledge helps each new generation of elephants play their part in shaping the land, carrying on the role of gardener that's so essential to their ecosystem.

The elephants' impact on their environment benefits not only plants and animals but also humans. In regions where elephants live, their actions support healthy forests and grasslands, which help prevent soil erosion, store carbon, and provide resources like clean water and fertile land. Healthy ecosystems also support agriculture, allowing local communities to grow crops and raise livestock. By keeping the environment balanced, elephants indirectly help people who depend on the land for food and income. In this way, elephants are not only guardians of their habitats but also allies to the communities that live nearby.

Despite their positive impact, elephants face challenges that make it hard for them to continue their important work. Habitat loss, poaching, and conflicts with humans threaten their populations and, in turn, the health of the ecosystems they care for. Conservation efforts around the world are focused on protecting elephants and ensuring they have the space they need to thrive. By preserving elephant habitats and supporting conservation, people are helping to maintain the balance that elephants create in their role as nature's gardeners.

5

ELEPHANT INTELLIGENCE

Elephants are known for their size and strength, but one of their most impressive features is something you can't see: their intelligence. An elephant's brain is huge—three to four times larger than a human's—and it's packed with the same kinds of neurons that help us think, feel, and problem-solve. Over the years, scientists have observed elephants doing things that prove just how smart they are, from using tools to solve problems to showing empathy and understanding emotions. These gentle giants are truly some of the most intelligent animals on Earth.

One of the most amazing ways elephants show their intelligence is through problem-solving. They can figure out how to overcome challenges in their environment, and they often do it in creative ways. Imagine an elephant coming across a barrier, like a log blocking its path to food or water. Instead of simply giving up, the elephant might try different approaches, such as moving the log with its trunk or stepping over it carefully. Their patience and determination allow them to work through problems without getting discouraged, and they often find a solution.

Elephants also demonstrate their intelligence through tool use, something that we typically associate with animals like chimpanzees or even humans. In the wild, elephants have been seen using branches to scratch those hard-to-reach spots or to swat away flies. They might break off a branch with their trunk, strip off the leaves, and use it just like we might use a back-scratcher. This simple act shows that elephants can use objects around them in new ways to make life more comfortable. It's not something they're born knowing; it's something they learn by observing others and experimenting on their own.

Water is another area where elephants show their problem-solving skills. Elephants need a lot of water every day, and in dry seasons, water sources can be hard to find. If a riverbed has dried up, elephants might dig into the ground with their trunks and tusks to reach the groundwater below. By creating a small well, they not only provide water for themselves but also for other animals in the area. This ability to locate and access hidden water sources is a testament to their intelligence and adaptability. They remember where waterholes are from season to season, which is a crucial survival skill in the wild.

Elephants also use tools for more complex tasks, especially when they're in captivity or close to humans. In some cases, elephants have learned to unhook latches or untie knots to access food or get out of enclosures. They use their trunks almost like hands, carefully manipulating objects to achieve their goal. This type of behavior shows not only intelligence but also a high level of curiosity and willingness to explore new ways of doing things. It's as if they're always asking themselves, "What else can I do with this?"

One famous example of elephant intelligence involves their ability to recognize themselves in a mirror. Most animals, when they see their reflection, don't understand that they're looking at themselves. But elephants have passed the "mirror test," a classic experiment used to test self-awareness in animals. When scientists placed a mark on an elephant's forehead that could only be seen in a mirror, the elephant used its trunk to touch the mark, showing that it understood the reflection was itself. This kind of self-recognition is rare in the animal kingdom and suggests that elephants have a complex sense of self.

Their intelligence goes beyond just practical skills; elephants also display an incredible emotional intelligence. They form strong social bonds, show empathy, and can even understand when other elephants are in distress. If a member of the herd is injured or upset, other elephants will gather around, offering comfort by touching it with their trunks or staying close. This behavior shows that elephants are capable of understanding the feelings of others, something that requires a high level of emotional intelligence.

Elephants' memory is another fascinating aspect of their intelligence. They are known for their remarkable ability to remember things for years, even decades. This isn't just a fun fact; it's a crucial skill for their survival. Matriarchs—the oldest and most experienced female elephants—remember the locations of waterholes and food sources, and they lead the herd to these places when resources are scarce. Elephants also remember other individuals, recognizing family members even after long periods apart. They can remember specific humans too, distinguishing between people who have treated them kindly and those who have posed a threat. This long-term memory helps them make decisions about where to go and who to trust.

Another example of problem-solving comes from how elephants protect themselves from the hot sun. On hot days, elephants often cover their backs with mud, which acts as a natural sunscreen and keeps their skin from drying out. To do this, they use their trunks to scoop mud and throw it over their bodies, carefully covering areas that are most exposed to the sun. This is an example of problem-solving in the natural world—figuring out a way to stay cool and protect their skin using what's available in their surroundings.

In captivity, elephants have also demonstrated their problem-solving abilities by working together. There are stories of elephants teaming up to complete tasks that would be difficult or impossible for a single elephant. For instance, two elephants might pull on opposite ends of a rope to move a heavy object, using teamwork to achieve a shared goal. This cooperative behavior is rare among animals and shows that elephants can not only solve problems but also work together to do so, understanding that their combined efforts can achieve something bigger.

One story from a research study involved an elephant figuring out how to retrieve food placed just out of reach. In a clever twist, the elephant learned to move a large block into position, step onto it, and reach the food that was previously too high. This behavior was not taught; the elephant figured it out on its own through trial and error, showing an ability to think creatively and plan ahead.

In areas where people and elephants share space, elephants have even adapted their behavior to avoid conflicts. For example, some elephants in Africa have learned to avoid areas with beehives, as they dislike the sound of buzzing bees. Farmers have started using beehive fences to protect their crops, as elephants naturally steer clear of these areas. This shows that elephants can adapt their behavior based on past experiences, learning to associate bees with danger and adjusting their movements to stay safe.

What makes elephants' intelligence so extraordinary is not just their ability to solve problems, but also their curiosity and willingness to learn. They explore their world with their trunks, test new ideas, and remember the lessons they learn. Each elephant builds on its own experiences and the experiences of others, creating a complex understanding of the world around them. Their intelligence allows them to adapt to changing environments, make thoughtful decisions, and form connections that last a lifetime.

Memory and emotional intelligence

One famous story of elephant compassion comes from the Amboseli National Park in Kenya. A young elephant calf named Olorien became separated from her herd and was at risk of being left behind. The matriarch of the herd, an older elephant named Echo, noticed the calf's distress and slowed the group down. Not only did Echo wait for Olorien, but she also used her trunk to guide the calf, gently nudging her back toward the safety of the herd. Other elephants joined in, surrounding the calf to keep her protected as they moved together. This kind of care isn't just a mother's instinct—it shows how the whole herd takes responsibility for its youngest and most vulnerable members.

Elephants don't only show compassion within their own species. In 1999, in South Africa's Kruger National Park, rangers observed an elephant named Nana who repeatedly returned to a spot where a dying impala lay. She didn't harm the impala; instead, she gently touched it with her trunk and stood by for several minutes, almost as if she were offering comfort. While we can't know exactly what Nana was feeling, this behavior was extraordinary, showing that elephants can recognize distress in other creatures and respond with care.

Teamwork is another incredible aspect of elephant behavior. In the wild, you might see elephants cooperating to solve a problem, like crossing a river or lifting a fallen tree that's blocking their path. But one particularly creative example of teamwork came from a study where two elephants were tested to see if they could work together to pull a rope and get a reward. The trick was that the rope had to be pulled simultaneously from both sides to release the food. At first, the elephants tried pulling it on their own, but when that didn't work, they quickly figured out they needed to wait for their partner. What's even more remarkable is that they didn't just pull together—they took turns eating, showing fairness and understanding of shared effort.

Another heartwarming story of elephant teamwork involves rescuing calves in trouble. In the Tarangire National Park in Tanzania, a young elephant got stuck in a deep mud hole. While the calf's mother struggled to pull it out, other members of the herd gathered around. They didn't just stand by and watch—they worked together, using their trunks and feet to loosen the mud and create a pathway for the calf to climb out. It took hours, but their persistence paid off, and the calf was finally freed. This wasn't just instinct; it was a coordinated effort that required patience, communication, and a shared determination to help one of their own.

Creativity often shines through in the way elephants solve problems, especially when it comes to accessing food or water. One of the most well-documented examples of elephant creativity comes from elephants in Thailand who learned to use tools to reach food. A group of elephants was given bananas placed out of reach, with a stick lying nearby. It didn't take long for one of the elephants to figure out that the stick could be used to pull the bananas closer. This wasn't something they had been taught—it was a moment of pure innovation, showing that elephants can think through challenges and come up with new solutions.

Another creative behavior was observed in a sanctuary in India. An elephant named Rajan learned to unscrew taps to get water. When the staff realized what he was doing, they started turning off the main water supply at night to prevent him from wasting water. But Rajan didn't give up. Instead, he started experimenting with the taps during the day, learning which ones still had water and when. His persistence and problem-solving skills left the staff both impressed and slightly outwitted.

Elephants have even been known to express themselves artistically. In some sanctuaries, elephants have been taught to paint using brushes held in their trunks. While the training for this activity involves human instruction, the way elephants create unique patterns on canvas has led some scientists to believe they have an understanding of shapes and colors. While we may never know if they truly appreciate art the way humans do, their ability to learn and perform such complex tasks is another example of their intelligence and creativity.

6

ELEPHANTS AND HUMANS

Elephants have captured the imaginations of people all over the world for thousands of years. With their size, strength, and gentle nature, they have inspired countless stories, artworks, and beliefs. From ancient myths to religious symbols, elephants hold a special place in many cultures. They are more than just animals—they are symbols of wisdom, power, and even luck, woven into the stories people tell to understand the world around them.

In India, elephants are deeply connected to religion and spirituality. One of the most beloved Hindu gods, Ganesha, has the head of an elephant and the body of a human. Ganesha is known as the remover of obstacles and the god of beginnings, often prayed to when people start new ventures or need guidance. You'll find statues of Ganesha everywhere in India, from temples to homes, often with his kind, elephant face and a trunk curled to one side. His image is a reminder of strength, wisdom, and the ability to overcome challenges.

In Buddhist traditions, elephants are symbols of patience and strength. They are also associated with mental clarity and focus. The story of the white elephant is an important one in Buddhism. It's said that before the Buddha was born, his mother, Queen Maya, dreamed of a white elephant carrying a lotus flower, a symbol of purity. This dream was seen as a sign that her child would grow up to be a great leader or spiritual teacher. To this day, white elephants are considered sacred in many Buddhist cultures, especially in countries like Thailand and Myanmar, where they are seen as symbols of prosperity and good fortune.

In African cultures, elephants are often seen as wise and noble creatures. In some traditions, they are thought to carry the spirits of ancestors, acting as guardians of the land. Stories and folktales often portray elephants as kind and intelligent, solving problems or helping others in need. For example, in some African myths, elephants are depicted as leaders who bring communities together, reflecting their real-life role as protectors and guides within their herds.

Elephants also appear in the myths and legends of Southeast Asia. In Thailand, they are considered national symbols and are closely tied to the country's history and culture. The white elephant, in particular, is a symbol of royal power. Kings would keep white elephants as a sign of their divine right to rule, believing that these rare animals brought blessings to their kingdom. Even today, the elephant is a symbol of Thailand, appearing in art, festivals, and even as a national emblem.

In ancient Greece and Rome, elephants were admired for their strength and exotic nature. While these cultures didn't have elephants roaming their lands, they encountered them through trade and during military campaigns, like when the famous Carthaginian general Hannibal used war elephants to cross the Alps. Elephants became symbols of power and wealth, often depicted in art and architecture to show the greatness of an empire. Coins from ancient times sometimes featured elephants, emphasizing their association with strength and majesty.

In China, elephants are symbols of wisdom and good luck. The Chinese word for elephant, "xiang," sounds similar to the word for "auspicious," which means something lucky or promising. Because of this, elephants often appear in Chinese art and decorations, especially during celebrations like the Lunar New Year. Statues of elephants with their trunks raised are thought to bring good fortune and happiness, and they're often placed near homes or businesses for protection and prosperity.

Elephants have also inspired art in incredible ways. Ancient carvings, paintings, and sculptures often feature elephants, reflecting their importance in the cultures that created them. In India, the intricate carvings on temples like those in Khajuraho often include elephants as part of the designs, symbolizing strength and fertility. In Africa, traditional masks and sculptures sometimes include elephant features, honoring their role as majestic and wise creatures.

In modern times, elephants continue to appear in art and popular culture. Children's books like *Babar* and *Horton Hears a Who!* tell stories of kind and clever elephants, bringing their gentle nature to life for young readers. In movies and cartoons, elephants are often portrayed as loyal, wise, or even a little goofy, but always lovable. These modern depictions might simplify their true nature, but they still capture the awe and admiration people feel for elephants.

Festivals around the world often celebrate elephants, showing their cultural importance. In Kerala, India, the annual Thrissur Pooram festival features elephants decked out in colorful decorations, carrying golden ornaments and participating in grand processions. In Sri Lanka, the Esala Perahera festival honors the sacred Tooth Relic of the Buddha, with elephants carrying the relic through the streets in a beautiful nighttime parade. These festivals are not just celebrations of elephants but also reminders of the respect and reverence people have for these animals.

Even in cultures where elephants aren't native, they have found their way into myths and art. In Norse mythology, for example, some scholars believe the god Odin's eight-legged horse, Sleipnir, might have been inspired by descriptions of elephants brought to

Northern Europe by travelers. This blending of stories shows how elephants' impact stretches far beyond the places where they live, influencing imaginations across the globe.

Elephants in myths

Elephants play an important role in conservation and tourism, and their presence is often the key to protecting entire ecosystems. These gentle giants inspire people around the world to care about wildlife and the environment. At the same time, tourism centered on elephants provides jobs and resources to local communities, helping both people and animals live in harmony. Their ability to draw attention to the natural world makes elephants a powerful symbol for conservation and a bridge between humans and the wild.

Imagine walking through a national park in Kenya or a wildlife reserve in Thailand and suddenly spotting a herd of elephants moving gracefully through the trees. Their sheer size and quiet strength leave visitors awestruck. Many people travel thousands of miles just to catch a glimpse of these incredible animals in their natural habitat. This kind of tourism—sometimes called eco-tourism—helps protect elephants by showing people why they are worth saving. When visitors fall in love with elephants, they are more likely to support efforts to protect them and the habitats they rely on.

Tourism doesn't just benefit elephants. It also

provides resources to conserve the land they live on. National parks and wildlife reserves use money from tourists to fund anti-poaching patrols, maintain protected areas, and create educational programs. In places like Amboseli National Park in Kenya or Udawalawe National Park in Sri Lanka, tourism helps pay for the rangers who keep elephants safe from harm. These parks often become sanctuaries not only for elephants but also for other species, from lions and leopards to birds and insects. By protecting elephants, we end up protecting an entire ecosystem.

Ethical elephant sanctuaries are another important part of conservation and tourism. These sanctuaries give elephants that have been rescued from difficult situations a chance to live in peace. In places like Elephant Nature Park in Thailand or Reteti Elephant Sanctuary in Kenya, elephants that were once mistreated or orphaned are cared for by people who understand their needs. Visitors can observe the elephants in spacious, natural environments, learning about their behaviors and the challenges they face in the wild. This kind of tourism focuses on respect and education, making sure the elephants come first.

At sanctuaries, elephants are often ambassadors for their species. They help teach visitors about the impact of poaching, habitat loss, and human-elephant conflict. For example, at the Sheldrick Wildlife Trust in Kenya, orphaned elephants are raised by dedicated caretakers until they're ready to return to the wild. Visitors to the sanctuary can watch the elephants being fed and playing together, while learning about the dangers they face and what's being done to help them. These experiences leave a lasting impression, encouraging people to support conservation efforts even after they leave.

One of the biggest threats to elephants is habitat loss. As human populations grow, forests and grasslands are often cleared to make way for farms, roads, and cities. This reduces the space elephants have to roam and can lead to conflicts between humans and elephants. In some areas, elephants wander into farmland in search of food, damaging crops and sometimes putting themselves at risk of being harmed by farmers trying to protect their livelihoods. Conservation programs often work to reduce these conflicts by helping people and elephants coexist.

One creative solution is the use of "bee fences." Elephants dislike bees and avoid areas where they hear buzzing. By setting up beehives around the edges of farms, farmers can gently deter elephants from entering their fields without harming them. This approach not only protects crops but also provides farmers with honey to sell, creating an extra source of income. It's a great example of how conservation can benefit both elephants and people.

Tourism also supports local communities by providing jobs and opportunities. In areas near elephant habitats, people often work as guides, trackers, or staff at eco-lodges. Some communities offer cultural experiences alongside wildlife tours, giving visitors a chance to learn about local traditions and ways of life. These jobs create a strong incentive to protect elephants, as they become a source of pride and prosperity for the community. When local people see the benefits of conservation, they are more likely to support efforts to protect elephants and their habitats.

Technology has also become a powerful tool in elephant conservation. GPS collars are used to track elephant movements, helping rangers monitor herds and respond quickly to threats like poaching or human-wildlife conflict. In some areas, drones are used to patrol large landscapes, providing a bird's-eye view of the terrain and making it easier to spot potential dangers. These technologies, combined with the efforts of local communities and conservation organizations, are making a real difference in the fight to protect elephants.

One of the most exciting aspects of elephant tourism and conservation is the opportunity for young people to get involved. Many sanctuaries and conservation programs have educational initiatives aimed at teaching children about the importance of wildlife. In schools near national parks, kids learn about elephants and other animals through storytelling, games, and hands-on activities. These programs inspire a new generation to care about conservation and to take action to protect the natural world.

The role of elephants in conservation and tourism

Elephants, with their towering size and gentle nature, need a lot of space to live. They roam over vast areas, searching for food, water, and places to rest. But as humans expand cities, farms, and roads, the wide-open spaces elephants once called home are shrinking. This problem is called habitat loss, and it's one of the biggest threats elephants face today. Imagine if your neighborhood suddenly disappeared, leaving you with nowhere safe to go. That's what's happening to elephants all over the world, and it's putting their survival at risk.

In Africa, savannah elephants once roamed across grasslands that stretched as far as the eye could see. These grassy plains were perfect for grazing, with plenty of food and space to wander. Forest elephants, on the other hand, thrived in the dense rainforests of Central and West Africa, where they fed on fruits, leaves, and bark. But as human populations have grown, these habitats have been cleared to make room for agriculture, logging, and urban development. When forests are chopped down or grasslands are turned into farms, elephants lose the places they depend on for survival.

One of the biggest challenges elephants face is finding enough food and water. An adult elephant needs to eat hundreds of pounds of food every day and drink up to 50 gallons of water. This isn't a problem in large, healthy ecosystems where food and water are plentiful. But as habitats are destroyed or divided by roads and fences, elephants often struggle to find what they need. Without enough resources, herds are forced to travel farther and farther, putting them at risk of exhaustion, hunger, and conflict with humans.

Habitat loss doesn't just mean less space—it also means more danger. When elephants' habitats are cut into smaller and smaller pieces, a problem called habitat fragmentation, it becomes harder for herds to stick together. For example, a road might run through an area where elephants live, separating family groups or cutting them off from important resources. Crossing these roads can be incredibly dangerous for elephants, as speeding cars and trucks often don't stop in time. In some places, overpasses or underpasses have been built to help elephants cross safely, but these solutions aren't available everywhere.

Another major cause of habitat loss is farming. As human populations grow, people need more land to grow food. In many parts of Africa and Asia, forests and grasslands are cleared to make way for crops like maize, rice, or palm oil. Elephants, naturally curious and always hungry, sometimes wander into these farms looking for food. To them, a field of corn might look like an all-you-can-eat buffet, but to farmers, it's a disaster. These encounters often lead to conflict, with elephants destroying crops and farmers trying to chase them away. In some cases, these clashes turn violent, putting both elephants and people in danger.

In addition to farming, logging is a major driver of

habitat loss. Trees are cut down for timber, paper, and other products, leaving behind barren landscapes where forests once stood. Logging roads open up previously untouched areas to development, further shrinking the space available for wildlife. For forest elephants, who rely on thick vegetation for food and shelter, deforestation is particularly devastating. Without the cover of trees, they are more vulnerable to predators and poachers, and their access to food becomes limited.

Habitat loss also affects the plants and animals that share the land with elephants. When elephants are forced to leave an area, it disrupts the balance of the ecosystem. Remember how elephants act as "gardeners" of the forest, spreading seeds and creating clearings that help other plants grow? When they're gone, the forest stops regenerating as it should. This impacts not just the elephants but also the birds, insects, and other creatures that depend on the plants they help grow.

Climate change is making the problem of habitat loss even worse. As temperatures rise and rainfall patterns shift, the places elephants live are becoming harder to survive in. Droughts are becoming more frequent, drying up waterholes and reducing the availability of food. In search of resources, elephants are traveling longer distances and entering areas where they might come into conflict with humans. This puts additional pressure on herds already struggling to adapt to their changing environments.

Despite these challenges, there are efforts to protect

elephants and their habitats. Many countries have established national parks and wildlife reserves where elephants can live safely. These protected areas provide a refuge for elephants, free from the pressures of farming, logging, and development. In Kenya, for example, Amboseli National Park is home to one of Africa's largest populations of elephants. Here, herds roam freely, and conservationists work to ensure they have enough food and water.

In some areas, corridors are being created to connect fragmented habitats. These corridors act like bridges, allowing elephants to move between different parts of their range without crossing dangerous roads or entering farmland. For example, in India, elephant corridors have been established to link forests separated by human development. These corridors not only help elephants but also reduce conflicts with humans by keeping them out of villages and fields.

Communities living near elephant habitats are also playing a role in conservation. By using methods like beehive fences or planting crops that elephants don't like to eat, farmers can protect their fields without harming elephants. Education programs teach people about the importance of elephants and how to coexist with them peacefully. In some places, eco-tourism provides an alternative source of income, encouraging communities to protect wildlife rather

7

ELEPHANTS IN DANGER

Elephants are known for their magnificent tusks, which are not only a part of their natural beauty but also a tool they use for digging, lifting, and defending themselves. But those same tusks have made elephants a target for poachers—people who illegally hunt them to take their ivory. Poaching for ivory has been one of the greatest threats to elephants for centuries, and it continues to endanger them today. The demand for ivory has caused heartbreaking losses, and while many people are working to stop it, the fight to protect elephants is far from over.

Ivory is highly valued because of its smooth, shiny texture and its ability to be carved into intricate shapes. For thousands of years, it has been used to make jewelry, ornaments, piano keys, and even statues. In some cultures, ivory was considered a symbol of wealth and power, and owning it showed that you were important or successful. This demand created a market for ivory, which led to the illegal hunting of elephants.

Imagine a world where tens of thousands of elephants are killed every year just for their tusks. This was the reality in the late 19th and early 20th centuries, during the height of the ivory trade. Elephants were hunted across Africa and Asia, their tusks taken and their bodies often left behind. It's a cruel and wasteful practice, and it had a devastating impact on elephant populations. In some areas, entire herds were wiped out, and certain species, like the African forest elephant, came dangerously close to extinction.

But why is ivory so valuable? Part of the answer lies in its rarity. Because elephants take many years to grow large tusks, ivory isn't something that can be easily replaced. Once a tusk is taken, it's gone forever. This scarcity makes ivory even more desirable to collectors and traders, driving up its price. Unfortunately, this demand has created a dangerous cycle: the more people want ivory, the more elephants are hunted, and the fewer elephants remain to grow tusks.

One of the most tragic aspects of poaching is how it disrupts elephant families. Elephants are highly social animals that live in close-knit herds led by a matriarch, the oldest and wisest female. When an elephant is killed, the entire herd feels the loss. Calves may be left without their mothers, struggling to survive without her protection and guidance. Herds may become smaller and less stable, making it harder for them to find food, water, and safety. Poaching doesn't just take an elephant's life—it tears apart the bonds that make their families so strong.

Efforts to stop poaching began many decades ago, and they've included everything from anti-poaching patrols to international agreements banning the ivory trade. In 1989, the Convention on International Trade in Endangered Species (CITES) placed a global ban on the ivory trade, making it illegal to buy or sell ivory across borders. This was a major step forward in protecting elephants, and it helped reduce the number of elephants killed for their tusks. However, the ban didn't eliminate the problem entirely. A black market for ivory still exists, and poachers continue to target elephants in some parts of the world.

Poachers use cruel methods to hunt elephants, often targeting them with high-powered rifles or setting traps that cause painful injuries. These methods are not only inhumane but also dangerous to other wildlife. Sometimes, traps meant for elephants catch other animals, like antelope or even big cats, causing unintended harm to the ecosystem. Poaching doesn't just threaten elephants—it puts entire habitats at risk.

Technology is now playing a big role in the fight against poaching. Rangers in many wildlife reserves use GPS tracking collars to monitor elephant movements and identify areas where herds are at risk. Drones are also being used to patrol large areas, giving conservationists a bird's-eye view of the landscape and helping them spot poachers before they strike. These tools, combined with the dedication of rangers and conservationists, are helping to reduce poaching in some regions.

Communities near elephant habitats are also stepping up to protect them. In Kenya, for example, local people are working as rangers and guides, helping to safeguard elephants while earning an income from ecotourism. These jobs provide an alternative to poaching, showing that protecting elephants can benefit both people and wildlife. Education programs teach communities about the importance of elephants and the long-term impact of poaching, helping to build a sense of pride in their natural heritage.

Another powerful tool in the fight against poaching is awareness. Many people around the world don't realize that buying ivory contributes to the death of elephants. Campaigns like "When the Buying Stops, the Killing Can Too" aim to educate consumers about the true cost of ivory. By reducing demand, these efforts make it less profitable for poachers to hunt elephants, helping to protect them in the long run.

There are also inspiring stories of elephants who have survived poaching attempts. In one case, an elephant named Tim in Kenya became a symbol of resilience. Tim had survived multiple attacks from poachers and even carried scars from spears and traps. Despite these injuries, he continued to thrive and became a favorite among visitors to Amboseli National Park. Tim's story is a reminder of the strength and determination of elephants—and why they're worth fighting for.

The scars left by poaching are deep, but they also show how important it is to protect these incredible animals. Elephants are not just victims of the ivory trade; they are survivors, adapting to challenges and inspiring people to take action. By working together, humans can help ensure that future generations of elephants roam freely, their tusks intact, and their families whole.

Elephants are majestic, gentle giants, but they are also wild animals with big needs. They require vast amounts of space, food, and water to survive, and their movements often bring them into contact with people who live near their habitats. As human populations grow and expand into areas where elephants once roamed freely, conflicts between people and elephants have become more common. This problem, known as human-wildlife conflict, poses a serious threat to both elephants and the communities living nearby.

Imagine a farmer who has spent months growing crops like maize, rice, or sugarcane. He relies on these crops to feed his family and make a living. But one night, a herd of elephants wanders onto his land, drawn by the delicious smell of ripe crops. To them, the fields are an easy source of food, and they may trample over the farmer's land, eating everything in sight. By morning, the farmer's hard work is destroyed, and he faces financial hardship. This kind of encounter can lead to anger and fear, creating tension between people and elephants.

Elephants, on the other hand, aren't trying to cause trouble. They are simply following their natural instincts, searching for food and water to survive. However, as more land is cleared for agriculture, housing, and roads, elephants have fewer options for safe habitats. Sometimes, their traditional migration routes are cut off by fences, villages, or highways, forcing them to detour through human settlements. When these paths cross, conflicts arise, and both elephants and people can get hurt.

One of the biggest challenges of human-wildlife conflict is that it often leads to dangerous situations. In some cases, people use harmful methods to keep elephants away from their fields, like setting up electric fences or using firecrackers. These methods can cause injuries, and frightened elephants may panic, creating chaos. On the other side, elephants are powerful animals, and a frightened or angry elephant can cause serious damage. When elephants feel threatened, they might charge at people or vehicles, leading to injuries and even loss of life.

Conservationists are working hard to find solutions that protect both elephants and people. One creative approach is the use of beehive fences. Elephants are naturally afraid of bees, and they avoid areas where they hear buzzing. By placing beehives around the edges of farms, farmers can keep elephants away from their crops without causing them harm. This solution not only protects the fields but also provides farmers with honey they can sell, adding extra income for their families.

In addition to beehive fences, some communities are planting "buffer crops" that elephants don't like to eat, such as chili peppers. Chilis have a strong smell and taste that elephants find unpleasant, so they tend to avoid fields with these plants. By planting chilis around their main crops, farmers create a natural barrier that discourages elephants from entering. This method is both effective and environmentally friendly, helping people and elephants coexist peacefully.

Another approach to reducing conflict is creating wildlife corridors. These are safe paths that connect different parts of an elephant's range, allowing them to move between areas without crossing through human settlements. In places like India and Kenya, conservationists work with governments and local communities to establish these corridors. By keeping elephants on these paths, people can reduce the likelihood of encounters with herds and help elephants reach essential resources like waterholes and feeding grounds.

Education also plays a huge role in preventing human-wildlife conflict. Programs that teach communities about elephants help people understand why these animals behave the way they do. When people learn more about elephants' needs and habits, they are more likely to support efforts to protect them. For example, children who grow up learning about the importance of elephants are more likely to grow into adults who respect and value these animals. Conservationists often work with schools, community centers, and local leaders to spread knowledge about peaceful ways to coexist with wildlife.

In some cases, communities are trained to act as wildlife rangers, working to protect elephants rather than harm them. These community rangers monitor elephant movements, guiding herds away from farms and villages when they come too close. By working with local people, conservation groups help create a sense of ownership and pride in protecting elephants. It also provides employment opportunities, showing that there are economic benefits to conservation.

Technology has become an important tool in managing human-wildlife conflict. GPS collars allow conservationists to track elephant movements in real-time, giving early warnings when herds are approaching villages or farms. With this information, people can take steps to prepare or guide the elephants away, reducing the chance of conflict. Drones are also used to monitor large areas, providing a bird's-eye view of elephant movements and helping rangers respond quickly to potential conflicts.

Why protecting elephants is important for the planet

Elephants aren't just important because they're amazing animals—they play a key role in keeping their environments healthy, which benefits the entire planet. These gentle giants are often called "ecosystem engineers" because of how they shape the landscapes around them. By doing what they do naturally—like eating plants, digging for water, and spreading seeds—elephants help maintain balance in ecosystems, supporting other plants, animals, and even people. Protecting elephants means protecting the forests, grasslands, and savannas they live in, which is vital for the health of our planet.

Imagine a dense forest where sunlight barely reaches the ground because of all the trees and thick vegetation. This kind of environment is a tough place for new plants to grow, especially the small ones that need light to thrive. But when a herd of elephants moves through, they open up the forest as they eat, knock down small trees, and trample tall grasses. This might sound destructive, but it's actually a good thing. By clearing paths and creating openings, elephants allow sunlight to reach the forest floor, helping a variety of plants grow. This mix of light and open space encourages new plants to take root, which in turn supports animals that rely on those plants for food and shelter.

Elephants also play a crucial role in seed dispersal. When elephants eat fruits, they often swallow the seeds whole. As they travel long distances, these seeds pass through their bodies and are deposited in different areas through their dung. The dung acts like natural fertilizer, providing the seeds with nutrients to grow. This helps spread plants far and wide, keeping the ecosystem diverse and healthy. In African forests, for example, elephants help disperse seeds of many tree species that are essential to the environment. Without elephants, these trees might struggle to reproduce, which would affect all the animals that depend on those trees.

Grasslands, like the savannas of Africa, also benefit from having elephants around. When elephants graze on grass, they help keep the grasslands from becoming overgrown or taken over by woody plants. Their grazing creates a balance, allowing a mix of grasses and small shrubs to grow, which supports different animals, from zebras and gazelles to birds and insects. By keeping grasslands healthy, elephants provide food and shelter for countless other species, making them central to the entire ecosystem.

Elephants are known for their love of water, and they help other animals access it too. During dry seasons, elephants often dig into riverbeds with their trunks and tusks to reach underground water. These waterholes they create become lifesavers for other animals, providing them with a source of water when other rivers or lakes have dried up. By digging, elephants make water available for a variety of species, from antelope and birds to smaller mammals like rabbits and squirrels. Even insects and plants benefit from these waterholes, showing just how far-reaching elephants' impact can be.

One of the biggest environmental benefits of elephants is their role in fighting climate change. Forests and grasslands are known as "carbon sinks," which means they absorb carbon dioxide, a gas that contributes to global warming. By helping forests and grasslands stay healthy, elephants play an indirect role in reducing the amount of carbon dioxide in the atmosphere. When elephants help spread seeds and encourage plant growth, they support these ecosystems in absorbing carbon, which helps cool the planet. Protecting elephants is not just about saving a single species; it's about safeguarding entire ecosystems that help combat climate change.

Elephants also bring people together, inspiring conservation efforts around the world. From rangers protecting elephants in Africa to scientists studying their behavior in Asia, countless people work to ensure that elephants have a future. These conservation efforts often lead to partnerships between countries, organizations, and local communities, creating a network of support that goes beyond elephants. When people come together to protect wildlife, they learn more about the environment, the importance of biodiversity, and the need to protect our natural resources.

In areas where elephants are protected, eco-tourism plays a big role in supporting local economies. People from all over the world travel to see elephants in their natural habitats, providing jobs for local communities as guides, rangers, and hospitality workers. This helps create a positive relationship between people and elephants, where communities benefit from protecting the animals rather than harming them. By giving communities a reason to protect elephants, eco-tourism encourages conservation that benefits both people and wildlife.

Organizations and people working to save elephants.

One well-known organization dedicated to saving elephants is the **David Sheldrick Wildlife Trust** in Kenya. This organization is famous for its work rescuing orphaned baby elephants, many of whom have lost their mothers to poaching or human-wildlife conflict. At the Sheldrick Wildlife Trust, these young elephants are given a second chance. The keepers, who act as substitute mothers, care for the calves day and night, feeding them, playing with them, and even sleeping nearby. When the elephants are strong and old enough, they're gradually introduced back into the wild, where they can join new herds and live free. The trust's work is inspiring because it shows how love, dedication, and patience can help heal even the biggest animals.

In Thailand, the **Elephant Nature Park** is another organization making a difference. This sanctuary rescues elephants that have been mistreated or forced to work in harmful situations, like logging or tourism. At the Elephant Nature Park, these elephants get to roam freely in a peaceful environment. Visitors come to learn about elephants, feed them, and watch them interact naturally with each other. By educating people about the issues facing elephants and giving the animals a safe home, the park shows how much better elephants thrive when they're treated with respect and kindness.

Save the Elephants is another organization with a unique approach. Founded by Dr. Iain Douglas-Hamilton, a passionate conservationist, Save the Elephants is based in Kenya and focuses on researching elephant behavior and protecting them from poachers. One of the organization's most exciting projects involves using GPS collars to track elephant herds. These collars help scientists and rangers monitor where elephants are and how they move across the landscape. By learning about elephants' migration patterns, Save the Elephants helps protect important corridors—paths that elephants use to travel between feeding and watering areas—keeping them safe from roads, fences, and other dangers.

In African countries, **Wildlife Conservation Society (WCS)** is known for its work protecting forest elephants in Central Africa. Forest elephants are smaller and shyer than their savannah relatives, making them harder to spot and study. The WCS team works deep in the forests of places like Gabon and the Congo Basin, gathering information on elephant populations and setting up anti-poaching patrols. Protecting forest elephants is crucial, not just for their survival but also for the health of the rainforests, which absorb carbon and help fight climate change. The work of WCS highlights how interconnected elephants are with their environment and why protecting them has benefits for the whole planet.

Many people who protect elephants work directly on the ground, often as rangers in national parks and wildlife reserves. **Rangers** are the frontline defenders against poachers, spending long hours patrolling the land, watching for signs of danger, and protecting elephants and other animals. Their job is risky and requires bravery and dedication. Rangers are often part of the local community, and their work goes beyond just guarding elephants—they also educate their neighbors about the importance of conservation and build trust between people and wildlife. In places like Kenya, Tanzania, and Zambia, rangers are celebrated as heroes for their role in protecting wildlife.

Organizations like **World Wildlife Fund (WWF)** and **International Fund for Animal Welfare (IFAW)** also contribute to elephant conservation by supporting research, policy changes, and community involvement. WWF works globally to protect elephant habitats and raise awareness about the threats they face. Their campaigns have helped bring attention to the dangers of the ivory trade and the need for international cooperation in protecting elephants. IFAW, on the other hand, runs programs to help reduce human-elephant conflict and to rescue and rehabilitate elephants in need. By working with governments, IFAW helps create laws and policies that protect elephants and the people who live near them.

Local communities play a huge role in elephant conservation. In many places, people who live near elephant habitats work together with conservation groups to find solutions that benefit both humans and elephants. One example of this is the **BeadWORKS project** in Kenya. Through this project, local women make beautiful beaded jewelry to sell. The money they earn provides an alternative to farming, reducing the pressure to clear land for crops. This means more space for elephants and less conflict over resources. By creating opportunities for people to earn a living in harmony with wildlife, projects like BeadWORKS show how conservation can improve lives on many levels.

Kids and teens around the world are also helping elephants. Organizations like **Jane Goodall's Roots & Shoots**program encourage young people to take action by learning about animals and the environment. Through Roots & Shoots, kids and teens start their own projects, from raising awareness about poaching to raising money for elephant sanctuaries. Some young people have even organized letter-writing campaigns to encourage lawmakers to pass stronger anti-poaching laws or to ban the ivory trade. These actions may seem small, but they add up to big changes, showing that anyone can make a difference for elephants.

Technology companies are even getting involved in elephant conservation. For instance, companies like **Google** and **Vulcan** have worked with wildlife organizations to develop tracking systems that use artificial intelligence to monitor elephant populations and predict poaching threats. By analyzing data from GPS collars, camera traps, and drones, these technologies give conservationists valuable information about where elephants are most at risk. The support from tech companies is an example of how creative ideas and partnerships can help solve complex problems.

8

HOW YOU CAN HELP ELEPHANTS

There's something amazing about elephants that makes people want to help them. Maybe it's their gentle eyes, the way they care for their families, or the important role they play in their environments. Whatever it is, elephants need our help, and there are plenty of things you can do, even as a kid, to make a difference for these incredible animals. You don't have to travel to Africa or Asia to help; you can take simple actions right where you are.

One of the most powerful ways you can help elephants is by learning about them and sharing what you know. When you tell friends, family, or classmates about elephants and the challenges they face, you spread awareness. You become an ambassador for elephants, helping other people understand why these animals are worth protecting. You might share fun facts about elephants' intelligence, their close family bonds, or how they're important to the environment. The more people know, the more they'll care, and caring is the first step toward making a difference.

Making a poster about elephants and putting it up at school or in your neighborhood is a great way to spread awareness. You can include interesting facts, beautiful pictures, and information about why elephants need our help. You could even organize a day at school to learn about elephants, inviting classmates to make their own posters or presentations. When everyone pitches in, it creates a ripple effect, reaching more and more people with the message of conservation.

Another way to support elephants is by learning about the things you buy. Ivory, for example, is made from elephant tusks, and it's one of the reasons elephants are endangered. By saying no to products made from ivory or other animal parts, you're taking a stand against poaching. Even though ivory items aren't as common as they once were, it's still good to be aware. You can also learn about sustainable products—things that are made in a way that doesn't harm animals or the environment. By choosing eco-friendly products, you show that you care about the Earth and all the creatures that live on it.

You might not have much money to donate, but every little bit counts! Many organizations that help elephants rely on donations to do their work. You could set up a "penny drive" at school or in your neighborhood, collecting spare change to support elephant conservation. You might ask friends or family members to contribute or even give up a small treat and donate the money instead. Once you've collected some money, you can send it to a trusted organization, like the David Sheldrick Wildlife Trust or Save the Elephants, knowing you've helped make a difference.

If you're feeling creative, you could make items to sell and donate the profits. Maybe you're good at drawing, and you could create elephant-themed artwork to sell at a school craft fair. Or, if you like making jewelry, you could design bracelets or necklaces inspired by elephants, using colors or charms that remind people of the jungle or savannah. By sharing your talents, you not only raise money but also inspire others to care about elephants.

One of the easiest ways to help elephants is by using your voice online. With your parents' permission, you could share elephant facts, photos, or conservation news on social media platforms. You could also participate in campaigns like #ElephantAwareness or join online events celebrating World Elephant Day, which takes place every year on August 12. Social media helps messages travel far and wide, reaching people all over the world who might not know about the challenges elephants face. Every post, like, and share helps spread the word.

Writing letters is another way to use your voice for elephants. You could write to companies that might sell ivory or products that harm the environment, asking them to think about the impact of their choices. Some kids even write to lawmakers, urging them to support laws that protect wildlife and ban ivory sales. It might feel like a small action, but companies and governments listen to what people say—especially young people who show they care about the future.

Reading books about elephants or watching documentaries is another powerful way to help. By learning more, you become even better at sharing information with others. Documentaries like *The Elephant Queen* or *Elephants: The Last Giants* show elephants in their natural habitats and the challenges they face. These films can be inspiring and give you ideas for how to help. You might even host a movie night with friends and family, turning it into a mini-awareness event where everyone learns together.

Getting your school involved can multiply your efforts. You could suggest hosting an "Elephant Day" or doing a class project about elephants and their role in the environment. Imagine your whole class raising money for elephant conservation, or everyone learning about ways to protect animals and the planet. Schools are great places to spread awareness because when kids work together, they can make a huge impact.

If you're interested in science, think about ways you could help elephants through technology. Many conservationists use tools like GPS collars, drones, and camera traps to study and protect elephants. You might not have access to these tools yet, but maybe one day, you'll be part of a team that uses technology to help wildlife. Learning about science and technology now could set you on a path to become a future conservationist, biologist, or even an engineer who designs equipment to protect animals.

Even little actions at home can help elephants and other animals. By reducing waste, recycling, and using less water and electricity, you help conserve the environment. When people use fewer resources, it means there's less need to clear land for new farms or buildings, leaving more space for animals like elephants. Small choices, like turning off the lights when you leave a room or using a reusable water bottle, might not seem connected to elephants, but they help keep the planet healthy for all its inhabitants.

9

FASCINATING ELEPHANT FACTS

Elephants are filled with surprises. There's so much more to them than meets the eye! Behind those huge ears, long trunks, and wrinkly skin are countless fascinating facts that make them one of the most extraordinary animals on the planet. Let's dive into some fun and surprising things about elephants that show just how amazing they really are.

One incredible thing about elephants is their memory. Ever heard the phrase, "An elephant never forgets"? There's actually some truth to it! Elephants have one of the best memories in the animal kingdom. They remember other elephants, places, and even humans they've met before. In the wild, elephants use this memory to keep track of important locations, like waterholes or safe paths. A matriarch, the oldest female in a herd, remembers where the best water sources are and leads her family there, even if they haven't been back to that spot in years. This memory is especially useful in times of drought when survival depends on finding food and water.

Elephants also communicate in fascinating ways. While we mostly hear them trumpeting with their trunks, elephants use sounds that are too low for humans to hear. These sounds, called infrasound, travel miles through the ground and air. Other elephants can pick up these signals with the sensitive skin on their feet. By communicating with infrasound, elephants can warn each other of danger, find each other when they're separated, and even send messages about where to meet up. Imagine having a conversation with your family from miles away without a phone—that's the power of elephant communication.

Another amazing fact about elephants is that they use their trunks for almost everything. An elephant's trunk has around 40,000 muscles—more than the entire human body! They use their trunks to pick up tiny objects, like a single blade of grass, or to lift heavy branches. Elephants also use their trunks like snorkels when they're swimming. That's right, elephants are excellent swimmers. They love water and will wade into lakes or rivers, using their trunks to breathe while submerged. Watching an elephant swim is a joyful sight —they often look like they're having a blast.

Elephants' ears aren't just for hearing; they're also like built-in air conditioners. In hot climates, an elephant's large ears help keep it cool. They fan their ears back and forth, creating a breeze that cools their blood. You can even see the tiny blood vessels in their ears if you look closely. This cooling system is especially helpful in places like the African savanna, where temperatures can get very high. When elephants flap their ears, they're not just expressing themselves—they're also staying comfortable.

Here's another fun fact: elephants love mud baths. They're not just rolling around in the mud for fun (although it sure looks like it); the mud actually helps protect their skin. Elephants have sensitive skin that can get sunburned, and mud acts like a natural sunscreen, keeping their skin safe from the sun. The mud also keeps pests away and cools them down. Watching a group of elephants splashing and rolling in a mud hole is like watching a giant pool party—it's clear they're enjoying every minute of it.

Did you know elephants can cry, play, and even show empathy? Elephants are known to comfort each other, especially when one of them is upset. If a young elephant is scared or in pain, others will come close and touch it with their trunks, almost like giving a reassuring hug. They've been observed mourning the loss of a family member, standing quietly around the body or gently touching it with their trunks. Elephants have complex emotions, much like humans, and they share deep bonds with each other. This emotional intelligence is part of what makes them so special.

Elephants are also very curious and can use tools. In the wild, elephants have been seen using sticks to scratch hard-to-reach places or using branches to swat flies. Elephants in captivity have even learned to pick up paintbrushes and make paintings! Although they're guided by trainers, some elephants seem to have fun experimenting with colors and shapes on canvas. These artistic elephants remind us of how playful and creative they can be.

Another surprising fact is how fast elephants can move when they need to. Despite their large size, elephants can run at speeds of up to 25 miles per hour. But, unlike humans or horses, they don't "gallop." Instead, they kind of speed-walk, always keeping at least one foot on the ground. Watching an elephant move quickly is impressive and a little surprising, considering their weight. African elephants, which are larger than Asian elephants, are particularly swift and can cover a lot of ground in a short amount of time.

Speaking of size, elephants are the largest land animals on Earth. African elephants can weigh up to 14,000 pounds (about the weight of two large cars), while Asian elephants are a bit smaller but still huge. An adult elephant eats hundreds of pounds of food a day, including grass, leaves, fruit, and bark. They spend up to 16 hours a day eating, which is necessary to support their massive bodies. Elephants need a lot of fuel, and their diet helps shape the ecosystems they live in.

Elephants also play a unique role in their environment. They're sometimes called "ecosystem engineers" because their actions change the landscape around them. When elephants knock down trees to eat leaves or create pathways, they make space for smaller animals to move through and for new plants to grow. Their dung is also full of seeds, which helps spread plants across the land. By doing what they naturally do, elephants help keep their habitats healthy and diverse.

One last fun fact: elephants can recognize themselves in a mirror. This is a sign of self-awareness, which is rare in the animal kingdom. Only a few animals, like dolphins, apes, and some birds, can do this. In experiments, elephants have shown they understand their reflection is not another elephant but themselves. This intelligence and awareness are part of what makes elephants so fascinating—they're capable of thinking, feeling, and even problem-solving.

Quick trivia to share with friends.

Did you know that an elephant's trunk has about 40,000 muscles in it? That's more muscles than humans have in their entire bodies! While we're getting by with around 600 muscles, elephants need all those extra muscles to use their trunk for everything from picking up tiny pieces of food to lifting heavy branches. The trunk is not just for show—it's an all-in-one tool for eating, drinking, greeting, and even hugging other elephants!

Here's something else that's pretty cool: elephants

have "fingers" at the end of their trunks! African elephants have two finger-like extensions, while Asian elephants have one. These help them pick up objects as small as a peanut or a single blade of grass. Imagine trying to grab a tiny item with only your nose—that's what it would be like for an elephant without these special trunk "fingers."

Speaking of size, let's talk about their ears. African elephants have larger ears than Asian elephants, and the shape of their ears even looks a bit like the continent of Africa! Their big ears aren't just for hearing; they also act as cooling systems. When an elephant flaps its ears, it helps cool down the blood that flows through the many tiny blood vessels in the ears, keeping the elephant comfortable in the hot sun.

Another amazing fact: elephants are excellent swimmers! They use their trunk like a snorkel to breathe while they're underwater. When elephants come across a river or lake, they don't just stop—they wade right in and start swimming. They can even float and paddle across deep water. For such a huge animal, they're incredibly graceful in the water, almost as if they were made for it.

Here's a fact that might surprise you: elephants can actually communicate using sound waves that humans can't hear. These sounds are called infrasound, and they travel through the ground and air, reaching other elephants that are miles away. By picking up these low-frequency sounds with their sensitive feet and trunks, elephants can "talk" to each other over long distances.

Imagine being able to chat with your friends across the whole neighborhood without using a phone!

Did you know that elephants can sometimes be "right-trunked" or "left-trunked"? Just like humans are often right- or left-handed, elephants tend to prefer one side when they use their trunk for delicate tasks. Next time you see a video of an elephant picking something up, try to notice which side it favors. It's like discovering that elephants have their own unique "personalities" in how they use their trunks.

Here's something impressive: elephants only sleep for about two to three hours each night. That's it! Because they're so big and need to eat so much, elephants spend most of their day (and night) grazing on grasses, leaves, and bark. They nap standing up, but every now and then, they'll lie down for a good, deep sleep, especially when they feel safe. It's amazing to think they accomplish so much on such little rest!

And get this—elephants can recognize themselves in a mirror. Only a few animals, like great apes, dolphins, and certain birds, have shown this ability. In studies, elephants looked at their own reflection and even touched marks that scientists put on their foreheads, showing they understood it was their own image. This makes elephants part of a small group of animals with self-awareness, a sign of their intelligence and emotional depth.

Have you ever wondered if elephants cry? Well, they do have tear ducts, and they can shed tears, but it's not exactly like human crying. However, elephants do show emotions in other ways. They've been seen comforting each other when one of them is upset, and they seem to mourn the loss of a herd member. Watching elephants show empathy and care for each other is a reminder of just how deeply they bond with their family.

Here's a quick fact about elephant babies, or calves. When they're born, they weigh around 200 pounds—that's about as heavy as a grown adult human! But despite their big size, they can't do much on their own at first. Baby elephants rely on their mothers and the rest of the herd to protect and guide them. They even need help figuring out how to use their trunks, often swinging them around clumsily at first. It's pretty cute to watch a baby elephant learning to control that long, wiggly trunk!

Did you know elephants are picky eaters? With their powerful trunks, they can carefully select the plants and fruits they like best. They've even been seen peeling bark off of trees and stripping leaves with their trunks, like professional chefs preparing a meal. And they don't just eat anything—they know which plants are best during certain seasons, so they're skilled at finding the most nutritious food all year round.

Let's talk tusks. Not all elephants have tusks; it's more common for male elephants to have large tusks, while some female elephants have smaller ones, or none at all. These tusks are actually elongated teeth, and they grow throughout an elephant's life. Elephants use their tusks for digging, lifting, and even defending themselves if they have to. Unfortunately, tusks are also the reason many elephants are targeted by poachers, which is why protecting them is so important.

Here's a fun and fast one: elephants are the only animals that can't jump. That's right! Because of their weight and the structure of their legs, elephants aren't built for jumping. But they don't really need to. Their strong legs and careful movements make them excellent walkers, and they can cover long distances without tiring. Their walk may look slow and steady, but elephants can actually move pretty quickly when they need to!

And one more to wrap up your trivia knowledge: elephants have an excellent sense of smell. In fact, it's thought to be one of the best in the animal kingdom. They can detect water from miles away, which helps them survive in dry environments. Elephants use their powerful sense of smell not only to find water but also to recognize other elephants, detect danger, and locate food. Their trunk is like a built-in super sniffer, giving them an edge when navigating their habitats.

10

THE FUTURE OF ELEPHANTS

One of the biggest challenges elephants face is the shrinking of their habitats. As human populations grow, more land is cleared for agriculture, roads, and cities. Elephants need a lot of space to roam, and they follow traditional migration routes that help them find water and food. When these paths are cut off by new buildings or farms, it becomes harder for elephants to survive. In some places, conservationists and local governments are creating wildlife corridors—pathways that link one part of an elephant's habitat to another. These corridors allow elephants to move safely between areas, even if there are human settlements nearby. Creating these paths means people and elephants have to share the land, but it helps elephants keep their natural behaviors, which is vital for their health and happiness.

Another important effort in shaping the future of

elephants is tackling human-wildlife conflict. As elephants roam in search of food and water, they sometimes wander into farmland, leading to conflict with farmers who rely on their crops to support their families. To help both people and elephants, conservationists are finding new ways to protect crops without harming the animals. One creative solution is using beehive fences. Elephants don't like bees and will avoid areas where they hear buzzing, so these fences create a safe barrier that keeps elephants away from fields. Plus, farmers get honey from the beehives, giving them an extra source of income. Solutions like this show that when people think creatively, they can find ways to protect elephants and improve their own lives at the same time.

Technology is also changing the future for elephants. Conservationists use GPS collars, drones, and camera traps to track elephant movements, monitor their health, and watch for poachers. With GPS collars, researchers can see where elephants are traveling in real time, helping them respond quickly to any dangers, like poachers or sudden changes in the elephants' environment. Drones provide an overhead view, allowing rangers to patrol large areas without disturbing the elephants. These high-tech tools are making it easier to protect elephants and gather information that will help conservation efforts for years to come.

One of the most challenging issues for elephants' future is poaching. Although there are laws against hunting elephants for their tusks, the illegal ivory trade still threatens these animals. Poaching isn't just a problem in one place; it's a global issue, driven by demand for ivory products. However, many organizations and governments are taking action. Some countries have strengthened their anti-poaching laws, and there are international agreements banning the ivory trade. Conservationists and rangers work to patrol and protect elephants from poachers, and in some areas, local communities are joining in the fight against poaching. As more people understand that buying ivory means hurting elephants, the hope is that demand for ivory will drop, helping keep elephants safe.

Education and awareness play a huge role in shaping the future for elephants. When people understand why elephants are important, they are more likely to take action to protect them. Schools, community centers, and conservation groups often hold events to teach people about elephants, the threats they face, and what can be done to help. Kids just like you can be part of this movement, sharing facts and stories about elephants with friends, family, and classmates. Imagine if every kid who learned about elephants shared their knowledge—pretty soon, everyone would be talking about how to help!

The future of elephants is also tied to how we take care of the planet. Elephants are a part of their environment, and they play a big role in keeping ecosystems healthy. In forests, they spread seeds that help trees grow, and in grasslands, they create clearings that allow different plants to thrive. By protecting elephants, we're also protecting the habitats that many other animals depend on. In this way, elephants are like ambassadors of nature. When we work to save elephants, we're also saving a piece of the natural world for future generations.

Elephants inspire people all over the world, from scientists and rangers to artists and kids like you. They remind us of the beauty of nature, the importance of family bonds, and the power of resilience. In some cultures, elephants are symbols of strength and wisdom, and in others, they are seen as sacred animals. This global love for elephants has sparked many conservation efforts, from international laws to local community projects. It's amazing to think that people from so many different backgrounds are coming together for a common goal: a world where elephants can live safely and freely.

There is hope in the younger generation. Kids and teens today have access to more information than ever before, and many are already passionate about protecting wildlife. As more young people learn about conservation, the number of voices speaking up for elephants grows. The future may hold new challenges for elephants, but with more people, especially young people, ready to help, there's a strong chance that elephants will have the protection they need. One day, you might even work as a conservationist, scientist, or educator, helping shape the future for elephants and other animals.

How you can make a difference

Kids have a powerful role in shaping the future for elephants. Even though they might not be conservationists or scientists yet, kids can make a difference every day by learning, taking action, and inspiring others. The choices kids make, the curiosity they have, and the passion they show are all pieces of a big puzzle that could lead to a better world for elephants and all animals. Becoming a future conservationist doesn't have to wait until you're older—it can start right now with a few small steps.

One of the easiest and most important things kids can do is keep learning. When you take the time to understand elephants, their habitats, and the problems they face, you're building a foundation of knowledge. Learning doesn't have to mean sitting with a textbook; it can be watching a documentary, reading a fun article, or even talking to someone who knows about animals. The more you know, the more you'll be able to teach others and spread awareness, turning each bit of knowledge into action.

Sometimes, making a difference means thinking creatively. Maybe you're really into art, writing, music, or even technology—these are all ways to help elephants. If you love drawing, you could make posters or comics that tell a story about elephants' lives and why they need protection. Writers can create short stories or blog posts that inspire readers to care about wildlife. Musicians can create songs that celebrate elephants and their habitats, and tech lovers can use apps to track conservation news. Creativity can make conservation feel personal and fun, and it allows you to connect with people in unique ways.

Starting a club or group with friends who also care about animals is another way to make an impact. Together, you could organize activities like fundraising for elephant sanctuaries, creating presentations for your class, or even setting up awareness days at school. By working as a team, you can accomplish even more, and you'll be able to lean on each other's strengths. One person might be great at organizing, while another is a talented artist, and someone else might love public speaking. Together, you can find ways to spread the word and support conservation causes as a small but mighty group.

If you're interested in science, there are many ways to start exploring the field of conservation right now. You might join a nature club, attend wildlife camps, or get involved in local science fairs. Learning about ecosystems, climate, and animal behavior builds the foundation for a future career in conservation or biology. Some kids even start their own mini research projects, like observing animal behavior in their own backyard or identifying plants and insects in a nearby park. Every step helps you understand the natural world, and the more you know, the better equipped you'll be to make a difference for elephants and other animals as you grow.

Public speaking can be a great way to share your

passion for elephants. You could give a short talk in class, create a video presentation, or even write a speech for an event. By talking about elephants and their struggles, you help others understand why it's important to care. You don't have to be an expert to make an impact—just speaking from the heart about what you've learned and why it matters to you can inspire others to get involved too. Your voice is powerful, and when you use it to raise awareness, you're taking a step toward becoming a conservationist.

Kids can also make a difference by encouraging others to be mindful of their actions. For example, you could talk to family and friends about eco-friendly choices, like using less plastic, recycling, and reducing waste. Small changes can help protect the habitats that elephants and other animals rely on. You might even encourage people to support products that don't harm wildlife or to avoid buying anything made from ivory. By making these choices yourself, you set an example and show others how easy it can be to help animals just by being thoughtful.

Using social media, with the help of a parent or guardian, is another powerful way to spread your message. Posting facts about elephants, sharing conservation news, or talking about your favorite elephant documentary can reach a lot of people in just a few clicks. You could even start a blog or create a series of videos to teach others about elephants and conservation. Social media lets you reach people beyond your school or neighborhood, allowing your message to spread far and wide. By sharing what you care about, you might inspire someone halfway around the world to care too.

One of the best ways to prepare to be a conservationist is by supporting organizations that help elephants and learning about what they do. Many conservation groups have youth programs, newsletters, and even virtual tours of elephant sanctuaries. You could "adopt" an elephant through an organization that cares for orphaned elephants, receiving updates about your elephant and learning about its life. This connection helps you see the real, individual lives that are impacted by conservation efforts, and it can deepen your commitment to helping animals.

As you learn about these organizations, you might also come across conservation role models. People like Dr. Iain Douglas-Hamilton, who founded Save the Elephants, and Dr. Jane Goodall, who has spent her life studying and protecting animals, are inspiring figures who show how much one person can do. Even though these scientists started their work many years ago, their passion and dedication have created lasting change for animals and the planet. Having role models in conservation can encourage you to keep learning, even when the challenges seem big.

Sometimes, the best way to understand how to help is to spend time in nature. By exploring a forest, walking through a park, or observing animals near your home, you'll start to notice the balance of life all around you.

This helps you understand why it's so important to protect habitats—not just for elephants but for all creatures. Conservation isn't only about faraway places; it's about caring for every part of the natural world. The more you explore, the more you'll understand how connected everything is, and that understanding is a powerful tool for a future conservationist.

CONCLUSION: CELEBRATE ELEPHANTS

You might wonder, "How can I make a difference?" Every action, no matter how small it may seem, has an impact. Protecting elephants can start with something as simple as choosing to learn more about them. Read books, watch documentaries, and dive into articles about their lives, their challenges, and the ways people are working to protect them. When you learn about elephants, you gain a deeper connection to them and a clearer understanding of why they are so important to our world. By knowing their stories and understanding their struggles, you'll be better prepared to speak up for them.

Another action you can take today is to spread the word about elephants. Tell your friends, family, or classmates why elephants are worth protecting. Share what you've learned about their intelligence, their emotional bonds, or their role as nature's gardeners. You might even share a fun fact, like how they communicate using low-frequency sounds that humans can't hear. When you talk about elephants, you're helping others see them in a new light, sparking curiosity and kindness in people who might not have thought about elephants before. Imagine how many minds you can change just by sharing your love for these incredible animals.

Small daily choices can also make a big difference. Think about ways you can protect the environment right where you live. By reducing waste, recycling, and conserving resources, you're helping the planet as a whole, which, in turn, helps animals like elephants. Elephants need large, wild spaces to roam, and when we make eco-friendly choices, we're helping to protect those habitats. Simple actions, like using a reusable water bottle, turning off lights when you leave a room, or recycling, might seem small, but every effort counts. When more people do the same, these actions add up, creating a world that's safer and healthier for all animals.

Supporting organizations that work to protect elephants is another great way to make a difference. There are many groups dedicated to saving elephants and their habitats. You might choose to "adopt" an elephant through a sanctuary or donate a small amount to a conservation organization. Every little bit helps, and you don't have to give a lot to make an impact. Some organizations use donations to buy GPS collars to track elephants' movements, pay for food and medical care for rescued elephants, or support rangers who patrol protected areas to keep elephants safe from poachers. By contributing, you're part of a bigger mission, a global team working to protect the giants of the wild.

Another powerful way to help is to encourage responsible tourism. Many people dream of seeing elephants up close, but it's important to choose places that treat elephants with respect and dignity. If you or your family ever plan to visit elephants in a sanctuary or zoo, look for places that prioritize the well-being of the animals. Avoid places that offer elephant rides or shows where they're forced to perform tricks, as these often involve training methods that are harmful to the animals. When we choose to support ethical wildlife tourism, we're helping to create a future where all animals are treated with care and respect.

You can also take action by participating in awareness campaigns. Many organizations hold events like World Elephant Day, where people come together to celebrate elephants and raise awareness about their struggles. You can join these events online, participate in activities like sharing posts, writing letters, or creating art inspired by elephants. When you participate, you're joining a global community that's committed to protecting elephants. Together, each action becomes part of a bigger movement that is working toward a future where elephants are safe and free.

For those who enjoy writing, creating stories, articles, or blog posts about elephants is another way to make a difference. Words have power, and by writing about elephants, you're helping to spread their story to even more people. You might write a short story about an elephant calf learning to use its trunk or an article about the role elephants play in their ecosystem. Every word you write can inspire readers to care more about elephants and become more aware of what's happening to them. Sharing these stories reminds people of why elephants are worth protecting.

If you're part of a school or community group, you could suggest organizing an "Elephant Awareness Day." This could include posters, fun facts, videos, and maybe even a small fundraising event. Imagine your classmates learning new things about elephants and understanding why these animals are so important. It might even inspire someone else to get involved in conservation or take action to help protect wildlife. When you create these opportunities, you're making a difference not only for elephants but for everyone who learns something new.

RESOURCES

Elephant conservation organizations.

1. The David Sheldrick Wildlife Trust

Located in Kenya, the David Sheldrick Wildlife Trust (DSWT) is one of the best-known organizations dedicated to rescuing orphaned baby elephants. They care for young elephants who have lost their mothers due to poaching or accidents, giving them a safe home until they're strong enough to return to the wild. One of the ways DSWT helps young supporters get involved is through their "Adopt an Orphan" program. For a small donation, kids can adopt a baby elephant, receive monthly updates, and follow their elephant's journey. Learning about each elephant's story and seeing their progress can be incredibly inspiring.

Website: sheldrickwildlifetrust.org

2. Save the Elephants

Save the Elephants (STE), also based in Kenya, focuses on research, protection, and raising awareness about elephants. STE works to track elephants' movements, protect them from poaching, and study their behavior. Kids can get involved by exploring their online learning resources and joining special awareness days, like World Elephant Day. They also encourage supporters to share elephant stories and help spread the message about protecting these incredible animals. For kids interested in science and technology, STE's research into elephant tracking and behavior is fascinating.

Website: savetheelephants.org

3. Wildlife SOS

Wildlife SOS is an organization based in India that rescues elephants and other animals in need. They provide care to elephants who have been mistreated or kept in captivity, giving them a new chance at a peaceful life. Kids can support Wildlife SOS by joining their elephant sponsorship program, where you can help care for an elephant at their sanctuary. Wildlife SOS often shares videos and stories of their rescued elephants, making it easy to feel connected to the animals you're helping. The organization also provides ways for young people to learn about humane treatment and animal welfare, which are important aspects of conservation.

Website: wildlifesos.org

4. International Elephant Foundation

The International Elephant Foundation (IEF) supports elephant conservation projects around the world, focusing on both African and Asian elephants. They work on everything from habitat protection and anti-poaching to researching elephant diseases. IEF offers a range of educational materials and activities to help kids learn about elephants, conservation, and how they can help. They also run special campaigns that kids can join to raise awareness and funds for elephant protection. For those who want to get involved in a variety of ways, IEF is a fantastic option.

Website: elephants.org

5. Elephant Nature Park

Elephant Nature Park (ENP) is located in Thailand and provides a sanctuary for elephants who were rescued from hard lives in captivity. ENP is a place where elephants can be elephants—free to roam, play, and socialize with each other. They offer a virtual adoption program, where supporters can help care for an elephant by sponsoring its food and medical needs. ENP shares regular updates, photos, and videos of their elephants, helping supporters feel like they're part of the herd. This sanctuary is a wonderful choice for kids who want to support a loving, safe environment for rescued elephants.

Website: elephantnaturepark.org

6. World Wildlife Fund (WWF)

WWF is a global organization that works to protect many types of wildlife, including elephants. They focus on protecting habitats, stopping poaching, and reducing human-elephant conflicts. WWF's online resources for kids are full of fun activities, including games, videos, and printable fact sheets that help young conservationists learn more about elephants and how they can help. WWF also has an "Adopt an Elephant" program that supports their work in protecting elephants and their habitats. This is a great organization for kids who want to learn about conservation on a global scale.

Website: worldwildlife.org

7. African Wildlife Foundation

The African Wildlife Foundation (AWF) is dedicated to protecting wildlife and wild lands across Africa, with a special focus on elephants. AWF works with local communities to create safe spaces for elephants and provides education about living peacefully with these animals. They offer resources for young conservationists, including fun videos, educational materials, and campaigns that kids can join to help spread awareness. AWF's work is important for kids interested in learning about both animal protection and how conservation helps communities.

Website: awf.org

8. The Elephant Sanctuary in Tennessee

The Elephant Sanctuary in Tennessee is a safe haven for elephants retired from zoos and circuses. While this sanctuary isn't open to the public, it has a fantastic virtual classroom with interactive activities and live-streaming elephant cameras that let you watch the elephants in their habitats. Kids can "adopt" an elephant and receive updates about their elephant's life at the sanctuary. This organization is perfect for kids who want to learn more about the lives of elephants and how sanctuaries provide lifelong care.

Website: elephants.com

9. Amboseli Trust for Elephants

Based in Kenya, the Amboseli Trust for Elephants is the world's longest-running elephant research project. This organization studies wild elephants and works to protect their habitats. They offer educational resources, videos, and stories from the field, helping kids see what it's like to study and protect elephants in the wild. By supporting the Amboseli Trust, young people can help ensure that elephants have safe and healthy environments for generations to come.

Website: elephanttrust.org

10. International Fund for Animal Welfare (IFAW)

IFAW works globally to protect animals and their habitats, including elephants. They offer a range of kid-friendly resources, including fact sheets, videos, and activity books about animals and conservation. IFAW also has a youth ambassador program where young people can learn how to become conservation advocates in their own communities. For kids interested in becoming leaders in conservation, IFAW offers tools and inspiration to help them get started.

Website: ifaw.org

Exploring these organizations is like joining a community of people who all share the same goal: to protect elephants and ensure they have safe, healthy lives. By supporting them, kids can make a difference for elephants and become part of a bigger mission. Each of these groups welcomes young people and provides fun ways to learn more, get involved, and celebrate these incredible giants of the wild.

Milton Keynes UK
Ingram Content Group UK Ltd.
UKHW020028271124
451585UK00014B/I509